The Silent Storm

The Silent Storm

Marion Marsh Brown
and Ruth Crone

Illustrated by Fritz Kredel

BAKER BOOK HOUSE

Grand Rapids, Michigan 49506

The Silent Storm

To two of our greatest teachers
We dedicate this book:

Dr. E. C. Beck
Dr. Louis E. Raths

CONTENTS

I. Departure for Tuscumbia

Outside the Perkins Institute for the Blind in South Boston a gentle March snow was falling. Inside in the usually neat cottage room which Annie Sullivan had for six years called home, a more violent storm had struck. In wild abandon it had flung clothing, ribbons, papers, and books into grotesque positions in every corner of the room. Annie was packing. And in every available space between baggage and belongings were girls—little girls, big girls—their chatter adding to the confusion.

From the bed, where she sat trying to fold an ungainly ruffled petticoat, Annie peered through her dark glasses and threw up her hands in despair. "Girls, please! Run along, or I'll never finish. I'll simply never, never make my train tomorrow."

"Do we *have* to?" begged a small girl, leaning against Annie and lovingly smoothing the dress of a beautiful doll which lay on the bed.

"Yes, you have to." Suddenly a firm voice spoke from the doorway. Mrs. Hopkins, "mother" of the cottage, had heard the commotion. "I know you're excited about Annie's trip and her job. So am I. But we must let her get packed."

Annie looked up gratefully. There was so much for which she had to thank Mrs. Hopkins. Even now, Mrs. Hopkins had no doubt divined the turbulence within her heart and knew that she needed to be alone—not only to bring order out of the chaos of the room, but even more, to sort out her thoughts and emotions.

Indeed, they were in a turmoil!

First, there was the distressing matter of leaving all that stood for home and family—Perkins, Mrs. Hopkins, the girls.

Then there was leaving Mr. Anagnos, the superintendent of the school, who had been very good to her and who, Annie thought, had in recent months perhaps looked upon her with a special tenderness. He was still young, though he had been widowed three years. Annie herself had just turned twenty, and people called her attractive. "If it weren't for my eyes!" she said to herself bitterly. Always there were her eyes.

Most disturbing of all, at the vortex of the mad, swirling eddy of her thoughts lay the thousand and one uncertainties about the job to which she was going: the job of tutoring a blind, deaf, mute child; the job of unleashing the imprisoned mind of a seven-year-old girl, Helen Keller, who since her nineteenth month had known no contact with the world except through the sense of touch. How could Annie, painfully aware of her own meager education and barren background, hope to succeed at such a colossal task? How did she even have the temerity to try? She did not know. But she had made up her mind; she had accepted the challenge; she had taken the job.

Sudden rebelliousness churned within her. It was grossly unfair—this Keller child's imprisonment; the darkness that was always with the children at Perkins. Annie knew what it was to miss the flame of red-orange sunsets shading to purple and mauve, the delicate pink of a conch shell, or the glisten of snow crystals drifting to earth like homing moths. Not long ago she too had been shut off from such beauty.

She wondered if it were still snowing now.

She left her work and went to the window to gaze out on the white-frosted quadrangle. It looked like a well-iced loaf cake, she thought, and smiled at herself. Always thinking of food!

Just then the dinner bell rang. No wonder she was hungry.

The lovely doll still lay on the bed—the doll the children at Perkins had bought for her to take to little Helen Keller and which deaf-and-dumb Laura Bridgman, the then middle-aged resident of Perkins whom Dr. Howe had taught, had dressed. Annie would carry the doll in her arms.

She closed her door and followed the chatter to the dining room, feeling already a bit apart, even a little lonely. She sat at the table with the fifteen other girls from her cottage and looked around her nostalgically, seeing things none too clearly through her smoked glasses, for her eyes were not yet recovered from a recent operation. Her throat felt tight. She wasn't hungry after all, but she tried to eat so Mrs. Hopkins wouldn't notice.

Mrs. Hopkins did notice. She patted Annie's hand. "You'll be back," she said. "You'll come back to see us, I'm sure."

"Will you write to us, Annie?"

"Of course."

"She's going to get *twenty-five* whole dollars a month!"

" 'Way down South in Alabama . . .' "

The conversation swirled about her, but she only half heard. "Somebody should shake me," she was saying to herself, "for having qualms about the job when I wanted one so badly. Why must I always be so torn?"

She brought herself back to the girls and their gentle teasing.

Annie felt rather than saw Mr. Anagnos at her side as they rose from the table. From the tone of his voice she knew his black eyes were smiling. "All ready to go, Annie?" he asked.

"Oh, Mr. Anagnos, I was just going to go look for you to see if you would strap up my trunk. *It's* ready, at least."

"Of course. I'll be happy to. I wanted to see you a moment anyway."

They walked together back to Annie's room, the other girls discreetly lagging behind.

"It's practically running over," Annie said, pointing to the trunk. "I never thought that I should have so many clothes. And of course I wouldn't if it weren't for dear Mrs. Hopkins. She made over her lavender dress for me, and she made me this wonderful going-away outfit." Proudly she displayed a heavy gray woolen dress and bonnet as Mr. Anagnos closed and strapped the trunk.

Mr. Anagnos straightened from where he had been stooping over the trunk and fumbled in his breast pocket. "I have a little something that I'd like to give you before you go—just a little remembrance."

He drew out a small box and laid it in Annie's trembling hand. "Oh, Mr. Anagnos! Oh, Mr. Anagnos . . ." she gasped. Her cheeks flushed with pleasure as she fumbled to open the box.

"Oh!" she exclaimed. There was awe and wonder, and a question too, in her voice. "A ring! I've never had a ring! Oh, it's lovely!"

Annie heard the rustle of skirts and looked up in relief to see Mrs. Hopkins at the door.

"Look, Mrs. Hopkins! Look what Mr. Anagnos has given me."

Mrs. Hopkins looked questioningly at Mr. Anagnos, the hint of a frown between her brows. Rings usually meant engagements. She didn't want this for Annie now.

"Just a little something to help her remember us at Perkins," he explained.

Mrs. Hopkins' frown relaxed. She nodded and smiled.

"It's very pretty, dear. A garnet, isn't it? And such a lovely setting. . . . I just came to see if there was anything you wanted."

Annie pirouetted to the window and looked out into the dusk. "It's quit snowing," she said.

Mrs. Hopkins stood waiting, knowing there was more to come.

"Yes, there is something I want—something I'd like to do tonight, for the girls." Annie was always one to suit action to words.

Quickly she put on her wraps. She took the ring from her finger, put it back in its box, and laid it carefully in her suitcase. "Thank you again, Mr. Anagnos," she said and darted from the room like a jack-in-the-box whose spring had suddenly been released.

"She's a strange child," Mrs. Hopkins murmured, shaking her head but smiling fondly.

"She's no longer a child," said Mr. Anagnos. "She's a strong, capable young woman, but with a tempestuous spirit. I don't know. I just don't know what . . ." He left the sentence unfinished as he walked hurriedly from the room.

Not even Mrs. Hopkins was prepared for the surprise Annie had waiting for them when she came dashing back into the cottage, her cheeks ablaze with color, tendrils of her dark hair which had escaped from under her hood sticking out at odd angles with much the same uneven abandon that characterized her disposition.

"Mrs. Hopkins," she called, "may the girls come out and 'see' ?"

Mrs. Hopkins went to the door to look, first, for herself.

It was moonlight, and Mrs. Hopkins had eyes with which to see. She gasped. After a moment, she said in a hushed tone, "My dear! It is beautiful!"

She turned back into the cottage. "Girls! Girls!" she called. "Put on your wraps and come 'see' Annie's surprise."

Excitedly they donned coats and caps.

"Here we go, then," she said when all were bundled, and led them to the center of the quadrangle.

"There!" she said, laying the hand of the nearest girl upon the snow statue she had made. The other girls crowded around, feeling swiftly, excitedly, lovingly—the little ones asking to be held up—"seeing" through their fingers the beautiful woman Annie had fashioned for them.

"A Snow Lady!"

"Oh, she's tall, and beautiful, like a Queen!"

"And proud . . ."

"And she's going to a ball."

Annie had modeled a life-sized figure, graceful, lovely, the proud head held high and circled with a heavy coil of hair from which one long curl hung down over the left shoulder. She was dressed in a low-cut evening gown with a long train and carried a cape over her arm.

"She has a gift, a real gift," Mrs. Hopkins commented to Mr. Anagnos, who had joined the group.

"It's a pity she can't be sent to art school," Mr. Anagnos said.

"Oh, no!" Annie breathed aloud. She stood perfectly still in the moonlight, no longer hearing the sounds about her, only the voice within herself: "I would not fashion forms. I would not shape the snow. 'Tis more than this I want." Putting the rest of the thought into words frightened her. "Might . . . just *might* I sculp a soul?"

II. The Past Returns

On the train, seated beside the window with the doll for Helen Keller at her side and her suitcase at her feet, Annie peered vainly through the dirty glass for one last look at Mrs. Hopkins and Mr. Anagnos. All the excitement and anticipation were suddenly gone. There were left only misery and fright.

She heard, "All aboard!" The train began to move, and the few human ties she had were left behind. Annie, alone, cried without restraint.

At length the conductor came by for her ticket. She dried her eyes and strove for control.

"Kinda big to be playin' with dolls, ain't you?"

Annie managed a shaky smile. "I'm taking it to a little girl where I'm going."

"Phew! Tuscumbia, Alabama." He was casting his eye down the length of her ticket. "Goin' a long ways. You'll change trains for the first time at Philadelphia."

Reading the ticket, he shook his head, but he said no more at the moment. The girl in the dark glasses looked miserable enough as it was.

Annie untied the red ribbons under her chin and laid the grey bonnet on the seat with the doll.

Suddenly she was back in time to when she was ten and taking her first trip. There had been the same keen excitement, and then the sharp misery, but there the parallel ended.

That other time she had not been alone. Jimmie had been with her. Little lame Jimmie, with the "bunch" on his hip, her brother, age five, hurrying to keep up on his small crutches. Even now, ten years later, Annie's eyes filled with tears as she remembered the pitiful little figure.

That other trip had been in February; she remembered someone had said it was Washington's Birthday. She was staying with her father's cousin John Sullivan and his wife Anastasia. On this particular day Aunt Ellen had come over with Annie's little sister Mary, whom she was keeping. A hack had drawn up at the door, and in the shadowy corner of the hack Jimmie was huddled.

"You and Jimmie are going to Springfield. You're going to get to ride on a train!" Cousin Anastasia said to Annie. In a high state of excitement, Annie clambered into the hack to join Jimmie.

"Jimmie, Jimmie! We're going on a trip!"

Jimmie's wan little face lit up briefly with a smile.

Annie remembered that she had not even bothered to wave goodbye to Anastasia Sullivan and her children as they stood on the porch watching the hack drive away.

Anastasia had been good to her in her way, Annie thought now. At least she had taken her in when there had been no place else for her to go after those frightful months when she had watched her mother die of tuberculosis, had fought back fiercely against the drunken blows of her father, and had tried in vain to quiet Baby Mary and to keep Jimmie out from under foot.

As the buggy bumped its way through Feeding Hills, Annie looked this way and that in eager curiosity. She thought to ask the driver, another Sullivan relative, with whom Jimmie had been staying, "Where are we going on the train?"

"To a place where they take care of younguns that ain't got folks o' their own to look after 'em," he answered shortly.

Annie had wondered briefly about this "place," but the excitement of going some place—any place—had crowded out concern. With all there was to see on the way, it had seemed no time at all until they were in Springfield. Then the horrible big monster, belching black smoke and shrieking its terrifying blasts, thundered down the tracks toward them. Annie caught her breath and clutched Jimmie tightly.

It stopped with a screech. They were hurried up a little set of steps and into the dim insides of this huge and hideous thing that must be a train.

Annie's memories of the ride itself were less vivid. At first the motion of the train and the steady chug-a-chug-a-chug of the ever-turning wheels had fascinated her. As the hours wore on, however, she grew tired and irritable, and Jimmie, she remembered, had begun to cry. She could see even less then than now—only a fast-moving dizzying blur.

The train had stopped and started, started and stopped, and the children had at length dozed fitfully.

Finally the conductor had gone up and down the aisle calling, "Boston! Boston!" Annie, only half awake, wondered if this were something to eat. If so she wished he would give her and Jimmie some. They were very hungry.

The man with the booming voice came back down the aisle and stopped by the seat where she and Jimmie lay hunched together for warmth and comfort. "Here's where you get off!" he announced. "Come on! Get up! Get your things on!"

Annie struggled into her ragged coat, helped Jimmie with his, and with her heart beating hard and fast, followed the conductor.

They had stumbled down the steps. Everything seemed dark to Annie. "Jimmie, is it night?" she asked.

"I—I don't think so," Jimmie sobbed.

"Here, you younguns," a man's voice said. "Are you the Sullivans?"

"Yes," Annie answered.

"Then come with me."

Suddenly Annie's Irish temper had flared. "How do we know we're supposed to come with you? Where are you taking us?" she demanded.

"To Tewksbury." The man had her by the arm and was propelling her rapidly over uneven paving stones.

"You're going too fast for Jimmie!" she shrilled at the man, and he slowed his pace.

They had walked and walked until finally they came to a place where there were many horses tied.

"Where are we?" she asked the man.

"Boston," he replied, at the same moment stopping beside a big, black, enclosed rig.

Suddenly Annie thought of her mother's funeral. They had put the coffin in a rig like this to take her mother to the cemetery. She shrank back. The man's arms lifted her to put her inside. Suddenly she turned into a ferocious wild animal. Her arms flailed, and she kicked him unmercifully.

"You little demon, you!" the man said through clenched teeth. But he did not let her go. He flung her into the dark interior and lifted Jimmie in after her. The door closed. Annie pounded on it with clenched fists.

"Let us out of here! Let us out!" she screamed.

She could not budge the door, and soon the rig began to move.

Jimmie had caught Annie's fear and was huddled in a heap on the floor sobbing. Annie fell to her knees beside him and tried to comfort him.

"Never mind, Jimmie. Never mind. We're just taking another trip."

Suddenly a fierce feeling of protectiveness for this

lame little brother had taken possession of her. She had never felt this way before. She had never felt anything like this way before. The anger, even the fear, drained from her.

"I'll take care of you, Jimmie. Don't cry. Sister will take care of you."

Comforted by the tone of her voice and her arms suddenly holding him tight, Jimmie gradually ceased to sob, and at last he slept. But Annie did not sleep. Her thoughts churned. "Where are they taking us? Tewksbury, the man said. Is that the name of a cemetery? What are they going to do with us?" A fierce hatred for her drunken father tore at her. "Nobody wants us! But I'll take care of you, Jimmie! I won't let them hurt you!"

Suddenly she realized that they were no longer moving. She picked Jimmie up and held him in her arms, but she had hurt his lame hip and he cried out. The door of the conveyance opened, and the man said, "Here we are. I'll take him."

"Oh, no you won't!" Annie spat out at him.

"I just want to help you down," the man said placatingly. "We're here. We're at Tewksbury. How'd you like your ride in the Black Maria?"

Annie had been in no mood to be placated. She had stood defiantly holding Jimmie, refusing to budge.

"Come here, Jake," the man called, and from somewhere another man appeared. "We've got a wild animal on our hands. I need some help."

24

Two of them were too much for her, and Annie found herself on the ground, but she still held Jimmie.

"He's kind of heavy, ain't he?"

One of the men offered Jimmie's crutches.

Annie stood looking about her. They seemed to be in the country or on the edge of a small town, but not in a cemetery. This calmed her fears, and she tried to bring into focus the building before which they stood. It was a large, shabby, grey frame house—yet very large for a house, she thought.

"Tewksbury?" she asked of the man who was guiding them up the battered steps and onto a rickety porch.

"Tewksbury Almshouse," he said, pushing open the door.

"The state poor house," the man who had come to help him supplemented.

It meant nothing to Annie. But at least they were inside out of the cold. They had not been dumped in a cemetery. And Jimmie was with her. No one could take him from her. She clutched him tightly as a man at a desk started asking her questions.

A rat ran across the bare boards of the floor. Annie's eyes followed it, but she was not alarmed. She had seen rats before. She answered the man's questions automatically, and he wrote down the answers.

"And when was *he* born?" he asked, pointing to Jimmie.

Just then a piercing, eerie scream, half shriek, half wail, rent the air, and Annie's eyes grew big.

25

Her glance darted quickly to the door across the room. "Come on! Come on!" the man said impatiently. "We have: 'James Sullivan, birthplace, Feeding Hills, Massachusetts.' Now what's his date of birth?"

III. Jimmie

Even now, as Annie's thoughts kept time to the revolving wheels of the train which was carrying her on the first lap of her journey to Helen Keller in Tuscumbia, Alabama, she could feel the chill of fear that had gone up her spine at the shriek of the insane woman ten years ago at Tewksbury.

This terror had been nothing compared to the paralyzing fear which had gripped her at the next words of the man behind the almshouse desk. He had finished filling in the blank and had summoned an attendant by the simple expedient of bawling, "George!" To the man who had shuffled in he said, "You take the boy to the men's ward. I'll take the girl up to the women's."

For a moment Annie had stood literally frozen with fear. Then Jimmie screamed, "No! No! Annie!" The sound roused her to action, and she turned into a fierce young tigress. With all her strength, she tore at the arm of the man who was gripping Jimmie's shoulder. Unable to break his hold, she clamped her teeth on his dirty wrist and bit down with all her might.

With a yelp of pain, the man let go.

In a flash she was holding Jimmie tightly in her own arms, and she turned savagely to the first man. Jimmie was clinging to her, shaking with a chill; his crutches were forgotten and went clattering to the floor, so that she must hold him from falling. He was sobbing and gasping. "I want to go with Annie! I want to go with Annie!" She had no time to try to comfort him. All she could do was to hold him fiercely against her wildly beating heart. "You can't! You can't!" she shrilled at the man. "I won't let you! I'll kill you! I . . ." Her fear and her anger were choking her. Her breath heaved in her chest.

Then something, perhaps the fact that she realized the man had made no move, made her peer closely into his face. What she saw there gave her courage and of the instant caused her to change her tactics. "Oh, please, Mister," she began to plead. "He's sick, and he's so little, and he *has* to have me to take care of him. Please. We'll do anything, only let me keep him with me. He'll die if . . ."

"He wouldn't be the first one," tersely put in the attendant, who was sullenly nursing his throbbing wrist.

The man who had been at the desk, the man Annie instinctively felt was the one who mattered, had still said no word.

Suddenly she saw that Jimmie was going to be sick— that very instant. Her plea was interrupted. She held his head as he vomited, then wiped his mouth, and laid him gently on a battered old leather couch which stood against the wall.

"Clean it up," the man said to the attendant. Then he sat down on the couch beside Annie, where, like a watchdog, she had taken up her position by Jimmie.

"It's against the rules," he said, "but there's a point even here. . . . You say he's five. . . . He doesn't look it."

Suddenly Annie caught a different tone in his voice. "We could put an apron on him . . ." he mused.

"Oh, *yes!*" Annie cried. "And let him go with me— with the women, you mean. Oh, Jimmie, you'd *love* to wear an apron, wouldn't you?"

"No," Jimmie said feebly.

Annie laughed aloud in her excitement.

"Listen to him," she said. "Of course he'll wear an apron, Sir. Then you will let him stay with me?"

The man sighed and stood. "We'll see what we can do," he said. "You wait here."

Annie relived the relief of that moment now, sitting on the train with no Jimmie beside her, only her aching, yearning memory of him, and realized that she had been reliving also the anger and the fear. Anger and fear. Fear and anger. How often had they gone hand-in-hand in her life!

Her mind switched back to Tewksbury.

After the man had gone, she sat crooning to Jimmie, stroking the hair off his forehead. "Oh, Jimmie, love . . ."

Suddenly it seemed as though her heart would burst with love for him. "Jimmie, Jimmie," she whispered, "we're going to be together. I didn't let them take you away from me. I won't ever, Jimmie. I won't ever."

Jimmie, weary and worn and ill, dozed again.

At last the man returned. "Come along," he said. "We've found a place for you for tonight. Tomorrow we'll make other arrangements."

What did he mean? Annie felt the fear begin to churn again at the pit of her stomach. "But you won't take Jimmie away from me—tomorrow?"

"No," the man replied, wearily. "We'll keep you together some way." He patted her shoulder as she struggled up, staggering under the dead weight of the sleeping child.

"I'll carry him," the man said, and this time she relinquished her burden, for she was no longer afraid.

For days that grew into weeks and weeks that grew into months—three months—she did not know fear.

The man had taken them to a narrow, dark little room which had no window. A kerosene lamp burned dimly. There was a bed in one corner, where he deposited Jimmie. There was a small altar in another corner. This much Annie could make out.

"I'm awful hungry," she said quickly before the man could get away.

"All right. I'll unlock the kitchen for you. I guess I'd better bring some food up to him, too." He nodded at

Jimmie, who looked very small and still as he slept.

He had led her through dim corridors to a big old kitchen and lit a smoky lamp. "There's the bread," he said. "The kettle's on the back of the stove. You can make yourself some tea." He left her.

While the water heated she tore off chunks of bread and stuffed them ravenously into her mouth. It was quiet in the kitchen; there was no sound save the crackling of the fire, so the mice and the cockroaches played hide-and-seek. Annie paid them no heed. When she had appeased her own hunger, she carried tea and bread back to Jimmie and awakened him to feed him. Then she fell on the bed beside him and was instantly asleep.

When she awoke, the kerosene light was out, and from the door came dim rays of daylight, filtered through a large room beyond, from which issued queer, eerie sounds.

Annie sat up and listened.

The high, wavering treble of a woman who she thought might be very old and who, she was equally sure, was Irish was croaking, "Rocked—in—the—cradle of the d-e-e-p, rocked in the cradle . . ."

There was an inhuman, continuous wail that made her think of the way the old hound dog her father used to keep chained by the door would bay at the moon on a clear winter night.

Just then a gong cut sharply through the odd medley of sounds to which Annie had been listening, and she jumped up. "Jimmie!" she cried. "Come on! Come on!"

As the tousled, dirty children emerged from the small room in which they had slept, an old crone with streaming hair pointed a bony finger at them. "Well, 'pon my soul!" she cackled. "Look what's a comin' outa the dead house. Reckon they're ghosts?"

" 'Dead house'?" questioned Annie.

The old one nodded sagely. "That's what. They wheel the dead-uns in there."

It mattered not to Annie. They had had a bed. Jimmie was with her. They were, she hoped, going to have breakfast.

"Breakfast?" she queried.

"Black bread'n coffee," the ancient one said and spat on the floor.

After breakfast, she and Jimmie had been assigned to cots out in the big room, where they would sleep from then on, among the derelicts, the insane, the diseased, and the dying.

Life became very exciting.

"Listen, Jimmie. Watch and see if you can do it!"

This was one of their favorite games. Jimmie was good at mimicry. When one of the insane women chanted some strange jargon, or another attempted to fly through the air like a bird, with a great waving of arms for wings, or another sat treadling an unseen spinning wheel, Jimmie would creep close and become an echo or a miniature shadow.

Annie would laugh loudly and clap her hands in glee.

"Look out, Jimmie! She's gettin' mad. She's gonna throw her shoe at you!" she would warn, and Jimmie would duck.

A stream of Irish oaths would follow while Annie screamed with laughter.

Her mind still at Tewksbury, she remembered how she and Jimmie had sat entranced, listening to the old, old women tell of the famine in Ireland, of the dead mothers and their dead babies lying side by side on their beds, mere skeletons—dead of starvation. These stories had intrigued her, and she had wept for the young mothers and their babies. Yet when another and another of the inmates of the ward in which she and Jimmie had taken up residence were wheeled into the "dead house" she did not cry. It was just a part of the day—or more often of the night.

When there were no corpses in the dead house, it was a playhouse for her and Jimmie. They made believe it was an Irish castle. Or they sat on its floor and cut out pictures from old magazines. Annie couldn't see the pictures very well. "You cut out this man," she would say to Jimmie, and Jimmie would say scornfully, "That ain't no man. That's a dog." "All right," Annie would say, unruffled, "cut out the dog, and I'll paste him up here on the wall."

She remembered the day the doctor had come to look

at Jimmie's hip and had found them there in the dead house.

He had looked about the walls, wildly decorated with all kinds of pictures cut in odd shapes and pasted at even odder angles. Suddenly he had guffawed.

"What's so funny?" Annie had asked defensively. "We're just puttin' up some pictures on the walls."

"So I see," he said. "So I see. Pictures of the living to entertain the dead!" He went off into peals of laughter again, and Annie was mildly insulted. Still, she liked to hear people laugh, so she laughed too.

As the days went by Jimmie cared less and less for their games of mimicry, less and less for cutting out pictures, less even for stories. He cried more and more. "It hurts, Annie," he would say, his small hand on the lump on his hip which seemed to be getting ever larger.

The doctor came oftener, but Jimmie cried more and more.

One morning Annie was helping him to dress.

"Never mind, Jimmie," she said. "The sun's shining. It's warm outside now. It's spring. I'll ask the doctor if I can borrow one of the wheelchairs. Maybe he'd let me take you out and wheel you up and down the walk today. You'd like that, wouldn't you?"

Instead of answering her Jimmie fell, screaming, in a heap on the floor. "It hurts! It hurts!" he cried over and over.

The matron came and helped Annie get Jimmie back

in bed. The doctor examined Jimmie. He gave him some medicine, and Jimmie grew quieter.

The doctor motioned Annie to follow him.

"You know, Annie," he said as they walked between the rows of cots, "your little brother can't live much longer. You should be glad because he . . ."

He never finished his sentence. A wild volcano unleashed its fury upon him, beating at his chest, stomping on his feet. "No! No! Jimmie isn't going to die! I won't let him die! Do something! Why don't you do something!"

The doctor was strong. He pinned her arms to her sides and carried her into the hall. "Annie Sullivan," he said through clenched teeth, "stop it! Stop that screaming! If you can't behave, I'll have you removed from the ward."

Instantly Annie was still. If she did not do what they said, they would separate her from Jimmie. She went limp, and the doctor released her pinioned arms. "That's better," he said, but perspiration stood out on his lip as he looked at the white-faced child who stood trembling before him.

Within the week Annie wakened one night to the sound of a cot's being wheeled to the dead house. Often before she had heard the whining and creaking of the cart wheels, but dimly, only half-wakened. This time she was wide awake. This time the sound terrified her. She could not reach out her hand to see if the cot next to hers was gone—Jimmie's cot—but something in her knew.

At last she had managed to turn her head, and in the dimness of the ward—the nightlights still burning, and the early dawn beginning to gray the blackness—she, who could hardly see, discerned a vacant space beside her cot. Jimmie was gone. Jimmie was dead.

She had begun to scream, and screaming in an agony of terror and anger and grief, shaking so that she could scarcely stand, she had stumbled the length of the ward to the dead house where she and Jimmie had so often played, but would play no more.

IV. Back to Tewksbury

As the train continued to carry Annie onward to Tuscumbia, her mind continued to carry her backward to the past.

The days that followed Jimmie's death seemed, in her mind, to be covered with a dense fog out of which only now and then a picture came clear, as when a breath of wind briefly lifts a curtain and objects which a moment before had been obscured stand out sharply.

One such picture was of the lilacs.

The matron asked her if she would like to cut some lilacs for Jimmie. She gathered a great armload and laid them on the pine box in which they had placed him. She did not cry as she stood there looking on him for the last time, but the storm of protest raged silently within her. Jimmie. . . . Jimmie was dead. Wherever she went the scent of lilacs seemed to go with her, and ever after that their delicate, dew-washed fragrance brought back the poignant pain.

Another picture was of a man gently lifting the small casket.

"Would you like to go to the burying ground, Annie?" the doctor asked kindly, his hand holding hers tightly to still the shaking that was all but making her teeth chatter.

"Oh, please, yes! Please let me go!" she had begged.

Then again a picture came clear.

She remembered the little path they had followed and the barren field to which it led. She could still see the hole and the pile of sand thrown up beside it. She did not cry as the little casket was lowered, but after they had shoveled the loose dirt upon it she threw herself face down on the small mound. Strong arms lifted her.

The next thing she could remember was sitting by the empty cot which had been Jimmie's—that night—the next; she did not know how long—longing desperately to die too. Jimmie was all she had lived for. He was all she had ever loved. There was nothing in life for her now.

She went through the days hearing nothing. But she could not go through the nights without hearing the sharp creak of the cots as they were wheeled away. She covered her ears with the ragged bedclothes, but still she heard.

"Annie, Annie," a gentle voice out of the night spoke her name. "Come here, Annie, and I'll tell you a story." It was the voice of Meg Carroll. Meg, who was so crippled she had to be strapped to a wooden frame, Meg, who probably suffered more than anyone else in the ward, but never complained. "Come close and I'll tell ye a story of the saints."

Annie did not remember that story or the others Meg had told. Perhaps she had not heard them. But she had heard the gentle, soothing voice, and at length she had slept.

"Talk to the priest when he comes, Annie," Meg begged her. "You'll feel better."

When the day came there was a rustle of anticipation in the ward.

"They've sent a new priest."

"His name's Father Barbara."

Annie looked up, incuriously, when the rustling came to a sudden, standing halt in the doorway. Dimly she saw a big man, and when he spoke she heard a big voice, but she also heard its gentleness. She looked more closely, trying to see his face. Her eyes followed him as he went from cot to cot in the ward.

By the time he reached her cot her heart had begun to pound. When he spoke to her she really heard what was being said to her for the first time since Jimmie's death.

"Annie? Annie Sullivan, your name after bein'?" There was a response to the warm smile on his face and in his voice. The faintest of smiles flicked across Annie's face.

"That's what it's after bein', Father," she said.

He lifted her chin. "Look at me, child. Can you see me?"

"Not very well, Father. So many bright colors keep jumpin' every which way between us."

"Bright colors?" he asked, his voice puzzled.

"Oh, yes, Father. They dance in front of me eyes all the time—red an' green an' yellow. They all go so fast that they make me poor head swim everytime they come."

She felt him peering at her.

"I know me eyes ain't pretty, Father," she said defensively. "Everybody says so. I'd be pretty if it wasn't for me eyes, though, wouldn't I? Meg Carroll says I would. But them!" She made a gesture to include the others in the ward. "They're mean. They say I'm a devil. They say Jimmie was a devil too." Suddenly she began to cry.

A big, gentle hand smoothed the hair out of her eyes. It pulled her head against a rough coat. It patted her shoulder. "It's a pity—a pity . . ." he murmured. Annie heard the compassion in his voice and cried the harder. "I'll see what I can do, Annie. I'll try to get you out of here—to a hospital . . ."

"Oh, no!" Annie screamed, sitting bolt upright. "I don't want to go away! Don't make me go away!"

"No, not just now," he soothed. "But let's think about it. I know a hospital where there are nice clean beds and kind sisters who laugh and make jokes and take care of sick people so they feel better. They wear starched white bonnets and their skirts rustle like a soft wind. I think you'd like it there, Annie."

"No!"

"And the doctors would see if they could help your eyes. Maybe they could make the bright patchwork colors go away so you wouldn't get dizzy. You'd like that, wouldn't you?"

"No!" she protested stubbornly. "No, I would not!"

"All right, then. Let's not fret about it." He rose, patted her shoulder, and continued on his rounds.

Annie half rose from her cot, then sank back.

The next time Father Barbara was due at Tewksbury Annie combed her hair as best she could and put on a clean dress. She did not sit on her cot to await his arrival, but stole quietly out of the ward and down the hall. When she heard his step she ran eagerly to meet him.

"Hello, Father Barbara! I was waiting for you!"

He took her hand. "You were waiting for me, Annie Sullivan? It's very nice to have someone waiting for you."

Hand in hand they walked down the dim corridor with its dirty walls and chipped plaster.

"Father Barbara . . ."

"Yes, Annie?"

"If I went to a—a hospital—would you go with me?"

"I'd take you there, Annie."

She had reached the door of the ward.

He squeezed her hand and released it. Her heart pounding, Annie went back to her cot while he went about his business.

When he had finished he came to her. "Let's take a walk, Annie. It's no fit day to be out, though," he added as an afterthought. "I guess we'll have to walk inside."

"We could go to the parlor," Annie suggested.

"Yes." Annie caught the distaste in his voice. At that moment a rat scuttled in front of them; in the dimness of the corridor Father Barbara almost stepped on it. "It's disgraceful, disgraceful!" he muttered.

"What is, Father?"

"The varmints. The filth. That ward. It's no place for a child. . . . It's a good thing you're healthy." Then his voice changed. "How about the hospital, Annie? I talked to a doctor who's a friend of mine. He would like to see your eyes and see if he could help you. You would get good food and care. It's the Hospital of the Soeurs de la Charité. Isn't that a pretty name?"

"What's it mean?"

"The Hospital of the Sisters of Charity. Do you know what charity is?"

Annie shook her head.

"It's love. The Sisters would love you and care for you."

Annie's mouth tightened. "No. Just Jimmie. Jimmie loved me."

"But Jimmie's gone, Annie. And, anyway, there's room for lots and lots of love in our lives. We need it. We need to receive it, and we need to give it. You see, Annie, God is love . . ."

"He let Jimmie die!"

"Annie! Annie! I know it's too much to expect you to understand. . . . All right. Just trust me. Will you do that?"

Annie did not reply. She broke away and ran back to the ward. Father Barbara did not follow her. He sighed deeply. "Another day . . ." he said to himself.

The day finally came, though there were many days between.

It was in February, a year after she and Jimmie had come to Tewksbury, that Father Barbara finally led her out the door.

She thought now how the Sisters of Charity had opened a whole new world for her—a world of order and cleanliness and lovely things for a little girl's hands to do.

Soon after her arrival Dr. Savory had operated on her eyes. She did not remember being afraid of the operation, or of the others that followed it. She remembered the bandages and how, once they were removed, there were no more bright colors dancing madly before her eyes. But she had been able to see very little.

At last Annie was well enough to leave the hospital.

"Annie," the Sister Superior explained to her, "Dr. Savory says you are well now. You have recovered from the operation, and while it didn't do all he hoped it might for your eyes, at least it helped."

Annie nodded. "I can help you now, can't I? I don't get dizzy any more, and I don't stumble so much."

"But, you see, Annie, we can only keep people in the hospital who need the doctors' and the nurses' care. You don't need that any more, so I'm afraid we can't keep you any longer."

Annie began to feel as if she were choking. "Where is Father Barbara?" she asked, her voice a hiss.

The Sister Superior reached to put a protecting arm

around her, but Annie pulled away. She stood breathing hard and looking defiantly at the Sister.

"He has had to go away, Annie. He's been called to another part of the country where he was needed."

Annie had to be sent back to Tewksbury. There was no place else for her to go.

V. To Learn to Read

"Philadelphia next stop! Philadelphia next stop!" the conductor called.

Annie roused herself from her reverie of the past and came back to the present with a start. This was where the conductor had said she must change trains. Her heart pounded now as it had that long-ago day when she had been told that she must go back to Tewksbury. She reached for her bonnet.

"This is where you change, Miss." The conductor was standing by her seat. "You just go to the ticket office inside the depot there and they'll tell you what train t' take. You'll have a while to wait though."

"Thank you. Thank you so much." Annie smiled up at him, picking up the doll that shared her seat.

"I hate to tell you this, Miss, but according to your ticket, this ain't the only change you're gonna have to make. You change again at Washington, D. C., for one, I remember."

Annie sighed. She had had no idea that getting to her job would be fraught with such difficulties, though she had anticipated plenty of problems with the job itself when she arrived.

The kindly conductor had been right. It was a long wait in Philadelphia, and even when at last it was over and she was on another train, the trip dragged endlessly. The passing of night into day and day into night, the five other changes she had to make from train to train, and the continually rising temperature were the only indications that she was making progress toward Tuscumbia. Her heavy, gray wool dress was like a tent that shut out every breath of air.

Her only escape from boredom and discomfort lay in the pictures in her own mind. As she did not know what lay ahead, she could only turn back to what she had known in the past.

When Annie returned to Tewksbury from her brief sojourn with the Sisters of Charity she was not placed in the hospital area where she had lived before, but in a general ward for women, across the way.

She remembered her surprise when she was taken to a building across the court from the one where she had been before. She had looked about her with interest. The first thing she noticed was that most of the women here were younger. Many were with child; that was the second thing she noticed. There were again the insane; it did not take her long to discover that.

"I'm Maggie Hogan," the matron had said. Annie looked her over with interest. She was a small woman with a crooked back. Her voice sounded tired and sad, but kind. Annie had come to judge much by voices. "This will be your bed."

When Maggie Hogan turned to leave, Annie realized that someone had been following them. A voice behind her said, "I'm Tilly." The girl must be somewhere in her teens, Annie thought. Tilly lowered her voice confidentially. "I'm going to run away," she whispered.

"Where you goin'?" Annie asked from the superiority of her twelve-year-old experience. After all, she had just been "out." When others did not want you any longer they sent you back to Tewksbury.

"Just away." Tilly waved her hand vaguely.

Annie shook her head.

As the days of her second sojourn at Tewksbury went by, she discovered that Tilly could be useful. Tilly could read!

There was a small library, Annie learned, in the Administration Building. She would entice Tilly to go there with her by pretending to help her plan her escape.

"You see, Tilly," she would say, "if they get used to seeing you going across the court like this they won't think anything about it. And then one day, when you're ready to leave and somebody leaves the gate open, like when they bring in somebody new or some groceries or something, you can just walk on out."

This never failed. Once she had Tilly in the tiny library, she would say, "Now read me what it says on the books." Tilly would read her the titles. "Let's take that one," Annie would decide, and they would stroll back across the courtyard. If Annie could work it she would get Tilly to read to her. This took a bit of doing.

The two girls would sit on the floor between the head of Annie's bed and the steampipes, their secret place, to plan Tilly's escape.

They would tie Tilly's few belongings up in a petticoat or a pillow slip, or whatever took Annie's fancy or was at hand. "Now, we'll put this under your bed." They would secrete the bundle between them and stealthily move to Tilly's bed. There were fifteen beds in all in the room, but Annie's and Tilly's were not far apart. "Now, that's all we can do today. Let's go read awhile," Annie would say.

Little by little, Annie would get enough of the story between the covers of the book so she could entertain the other girls in the evening by telling it to them. Most of them could not read.

One day she had said to Maggie Hogan, "I wish *I* could read. Tilly's so simple. She never knows where she left off, and I just know she leaves things out."

Maggie Hogan stopped in her busy routine and looked at her compassionately. "What's to become of ye, Annie Sullivan?" she asked with a sigh. "Ye ought to go to school. But ye can't see. There's that school, though, I used to hear about."

"What school?" Annie demanded.

"A school where they teach blind children," Maggie said, more to herself than to Annie. But Annie heard. She tugged at Maggie's sleeve. "Maggie! Maggie! Do you s'pose they could teach me?"

"Sure an' they would teach ye all right. Ye're a smart 'un."

"Maggie, where is it?"

Maggie shook her off impatiently. "No use thinkin' about it. I shouldn't of mentioned it."

"Why, Maggie? Why's there not any use thinkin' about it? I want to go to school. I want to learn to read like Tilly."

"But ye can't see!"

"Maggie, you just said . . ."

"I know. I shouldn't of said it. 'Twould be impossible, child. Impossible."

"But why?"

"Because, Annie, it would take money."

"Money?" Annie asked vaguely. Annie had never in her life felt as much as a penny in her own thin, wistful fist.

She did not forget the brief conversation between her and Maggie. There must be some way. If there were schools to teach the blind she *must* find out about them.

There was a pretty, blackhaired, blue-eyed girl named Mary who waited on the superintendent's table. She wore a crisp blue uniform and a white apron. Annie adored her.

When Annie asked her about schools she looked thoughtful for a second.

"There's the Board of Trustees coming to visit next week."

"You mean the men that eat at the superintendent's table and strut around looking important every so often? What about 'em?"

"I don't know, but I was just thinking . . ."

"You mean maybe *they'd* take me to a school?" Annie demanded, thinking of Father Barbara and the Sisters of Charity.

"Not *take* you, Silly. But maybe they'd know what you'd have to do."

Annie had stood looking after her with her mouth hanging open. Then she ran to find Maggie Hogan. "Maggie! Maggie!" she cried. "Men—men—Big Men—the Board of Trustees. . . . Mary says they're comin'. What's the name of that school?"

"What school?"

"The one you were after tellin' me about. The one where they teach blind children. Where is it? Tell me what you know. Please, Maggie!"

Annie looked back with tenderness on Maggie Hogan and her kind heart. No doubt she had thought she was only satisfying a child's mood of the moment, but she answered her. " 'Tain't far from here," she said. "Twenty miles or so. It's in South Boston. Let's see . . . Perkins, I think 'tis."

Annie dashed off. When she found Mary, she said, "Mary, promise you'll let me know the day they're comin'. Please! I'll do anythin' for you. I'll iron your aprons. I'll make your bed. Please! You'll know when they're comin' on account of the table."

"Yes, I'll know when they're after comin'. But I warn ye. 'Twill do ye no good."

"Then you'll tell me! You *will* tell me?"

"Iron my aprons and make my bed for a month?"

"Oh, yes, Mary! Yes!"

"All right, then."

In the days that followed, Annie had hardly been able to contain herself. Ominous whispers went about the ward. "They're investigatin' us."

"There's a man by the name of Sanborn," Mary told her. "He's the head one. Maybe ye ought to try him."

"How'd I know which one he is?"

"I don't know."

At long last the day arrived. Annie couldn't swallow a mouthful at dinner. Mary had slipped in and told her: *The men* were there. The superintendent was awfully cross, and he was going everywhere with them. She didn't think Annie should try anything.

Annie's heart was in her throat, but after dinner she waited quietly in the hall outside the dining room where the superintendent and the other help ate. Mary caught sight of her and shook her head. Annie slunk further back in the shadows and waited. At last the men came out. They did not see her, or paid her no heed if they did. When they were well down the hall she followed them, walking on tiptoe. She would wait until just the right moment. And she must work up her courage.

They went to the men's wing. She couldn't go there, but she waited patiently outside until they returned. They went across to the hospital wing where she used to live, and she followed.

Like a little shadow, she went where they went until it was late afternoon and they were walking toward the gate. Then she hastened her step and drew nearer. She was trembling all over. Her hands were wet. Now was the time. If she didn't do it now. . . Then the superintendent turned as he went to unlock the gate. He saw her. He frowned. He shook his head and motioned her back. Then, remembering her as "that blind girl," he realized that she could probably not see him. His temper was on edge after the scrutiny his establishment had been under-going, and he said sharply, "You, there! What are you doing here? Get back to the ward where you belong!"

But no sharp words could have stopped Annie now. Nothing could have stopped her. Having no idea which of the group of men might be Mr. Sanborn, she had flung herself on the man nearest to her, crying, "Mr. Sanborn! Mr. Sanborn! I want to go to school! Please! I want to go to Perkins, Mr. Sanborn! I want to learn to read!"

VI. "Big Annie"

All this Annie remembered as vividly as the day it had happened.

She had found another reader, Delia, an English girl. One hot afternoon the two girls had sat under a tree, Delia reading aloud from an Irish novel Annie had selected from Tewksbury's meager library. This was better than Tilly's reading. Delia didn't skip. But Annie's mind was skipping that day. She kept thinking about how she would like to be able to read like Tilly and Delia—to be able to look at a page and have the strange, squirming figures turn into the magic of words which wove a story and took you far away from the squalor of the almshouse. But she had to get her face almost against the page before she could see the figures, and then they would not stand still. How could she ever hope to decipher their magic? She sighed.

"What's the matter?" Delia had asked, putting her finger on the line to keep her place. "This story ain't sad. You're not listenin', that's what. And if you ain't gonna listen, I ain't gonna read."

She stuck out her lower lip and closed the book, but Annie, reaching out a hand to stop her, noticed that she kept her finger in her place. "I was just wishing I could read, Delia," she said. "Maggie said there was a school where they teach blind children to read!" Her voice was shrill with the intensity of her emotion.

Delia sniffed. "You can't never learn to read. You can't even see where you're agoin'."

As usual when she felt frustrated beyond endurance, Annie resorted to blind rage, and her fists flew at Delia.

" 'Tain't so! 'Tain't so! Don't you dare say it is so!" she shrieked.

Delia jumped up and started to run. Through the din, she called over her shoulder as she approached the women's ward, "Maggie's callin' you, Annie."

Annie didn't believe her. This was just Delia's method of escape. As she went flying through the door in pursuit, a grip of iron caught her wrist and brought her up sharp. "Annie, Annie! Quit your shrieking and come with me. I want to talk to you."

Annie respected Maggie. She followed meekly enough after the hunchbacked little matron, her rage suddenly drained from her.

Maggie took her to the cubbyhole that was called her office. It was stifling hot. Annie pushed the damp auburn hair off her forehead.

"Sit down, Annie," Maggie said. "I have something I want to say—and something that you want very much to hear." Maggie's voice softened.

Annie sat on the edge of her chair. "You don't be after

meanin'—that me father's finally come t' see me, do you?"

"No, Annie, not that, but . . ." Maggie saw the thin hands tighten on the chair.

She put her hand on the child's bony shoulder. There were not many people Annie would allow to touch her, but Maggie was privileged.

"Listen to me, Annie," Maggie said. "A letter has come from Mr. Sanborn about you."

"Maggie—am I going to school?" she breathed.

"Faith, an' ye may be," Maggie said, "if ye'll act like a lady. This letter says, 'Massachusetts School and Perkins Institute for the Blind are agreed to waive tuition for the ward of the State of Massachusetts, to wit, Annie Sullivan.' "

"What's it mean?" Annie interrupted frantically.

"That they'll take you even though you can't pay," Maggie explained.

"Oh, Maggie, I'm going to learn to read! I'm going to learn to read!" Annie shouted, jumping from her chair and throwing her arms around Maggie in wild abandon. Then she was out the door and running down the hall screaming, "I'm going to learn to read! I'm going to school! Do you hear, everybody? I'm going to learn . . ." She caught her toe in the worn hall matting and fell flat, the impact knocking the wind out of her in mid-sentence.

Nothing, however, could knock the wind out of Annie Sullivan for long. Especially not when the promise of school lay before her. "I don't care if my father *never* comes to see me," she said defiantly to herself as she got to her feet. "I'm going to learn to read!" She could walk alone, once she learned to read. She was sure of it.

In the weeks that followed, Annie's usual restlessness and impatience were increased a hundredfold. She could not wait. Why couldn't she go *now?* she demanded of Maggie. "Because school doesn't start until September," Maggie explained. "Anyway," she added, sighing, "you can't go that way. You've got to have some proper clothes . . ." Her voice trailed off. It would be hard enough for this wild colt of a child at best; it would be impossible for her were she sent in rags to associate with children who had homes and loving parents and tender care. Maggie decided that when she put in her annual requisition for bedding muslin, she would include two lengths of calico. Just maybe it would slip by unnoticed.

It did. Maggie was delighted. One length of blue and one of red.

Annie felt very fine when she climbed into the Black Maria which had brought her and Jimmie to Tewksbury and which was now to take her away. She wore the red calico and carried the blue in a paper parcel. This was the sum of her worldly possessions.

It was twenty miles to Perkins. "Twenty miles to heaven!" she said extravagantly to Tim, the driver, throwing out her arms as if to encompass all celestial glories.

Tim looked at her and clucked to the horses.

When Tim said, "This is it," and turned the team

into the gate, there was suddenly a lump of lead at the pit of her stomach, and the palms of her hands began to perspire. Tim pulled to a stop before the door of the Saint Washington mansion which had been made into a school, took Annie's hand to help her down, and said earnestly, "Don't never come back to Tewksbury, Annie. Leave it behind ye, now that you've got away. Forget all about it, and you'll be all right."

In the days that followed, Annie was to remember these words, for there were times when by far the easiest thing to do would have been to return to Tewksbury.

Feeling her way, Annie had found the door, pushed it open, and announced in a loud voice, with far more bravado than she felt, "I'm Annie Sullivan, come to learn to read." A dead silence engulfed her. Yet she felt the presence of others somewhere near. She put out her hand experimentally. She seemed to be in a large hall. Then she heard something like a gasp of amazement, definitely feminine, and turned in the direction from which it had come. "Just a minute," a young woman's voice said. "I'll call Mr. Anagnos."

"I've come to learn to read," Annie repeated. She sniffed appreciatively of the clean smell of furniture polish and wax. Then a door opened and a man's voice spoke. "You're Annie Sullivan?"

"That's me name as far as I know," Annie said. "Are ye gonna teach me to read?" The gasp came again. Annie turned her head in its direction with interest.

"No, not me. I'm the headmaster here. Miss Grey will just register you now and tomorrow we'll determine in which class to place you. Miss Grey . . ."

The young woman's voice said, "Yes, Mr. Anagnos. Annie Sullivan. Will you spell 'Sullivan' for me please?"

"Spell?" It was Annie's turn to gasp. "But I can't spell!"

"You mean you can't even spell your own name?" Miss Grey asked in unbelief. Mr. Anagnos stopped, his hand on the doorknob. "Register her in the beginners' class, Miss Grey," he said, and went out.

If Miss Grey and Mr. Anagnos had been aghast at the plight of Annie Sullivan, aged fourteen, the girls who were to be her schoolmates were astounded.

"You mean you don't have any nightdress?" they demanded when bedtime made it necessary for Annie to remove the red calico.

"Why would anybody want a dress at night?" Annie demanded defiantly. "Your drawers are to sleep in."

The girls giggled, but Annie told herself she didn't care. The smooth, clean sheets felt wonderful—like the ones at the hospital of the Sisters of Charity. "They've been ironed," she thought, running her hands happily over their smoothness.

Nothing was smooth the next morning, however. Annie discovered in dismay that all the other beginners were mere babies. Their prattling reminded her of Jimmie, and she was suddenly desperately unhappy and alone. When the teacher said, "And your name is Annie Sullivan?" Annie did not reply. She sat with arms folded and glared.

The little girls swarmed around, feeling this strange new member of their class. "Big Annie!" someone said. They all took up the chant, "Big Annie! Big Annie!" Annie's arms came unfolded. Her hands shot out, and the little girls scattered, screaming.

"Annie!" the teacher said sharply. "No pupil at Perkins ever strikes another. If you want to stay here you will behave like a lady."

Annie sat on her hands, but she didn't bite her tongue. "*They* weren't acting like ladies," she yelled.

"And keep your voice down." The teacher clapped her hands for order. "Children! Children! Let's come to attention now. Teacher has something very nice for you to do this morning."

Involuntarily, Annie's hands came out from under her and reached out. Surely the teacher was going to put a book into her hands! Now she was going to learn to read. She could put up with being with these babies. She could put up with their taunts if only the teacher would give her a book and teach her to read.

When the teacher reached her, however, it was not the hard cover of a book which she placed in her hands, but a handful of strands of soft wool. "We're going to start weaving some mats for our mothers," she said brightly.

Annie felt the softness in her hands and heard the cooing words; she threw the wool across the room and stomped to the door. "I came here to learn to *read!*" she shouted scornfully. "I want to see Mr. Anagnos."

"You'll see him all right, my fine lady," the teacher said, grabbing her by the arm and steering her down the hall.

Annie jerked away.

Then she heard Mr. Anagnos' voice, "What's all this commotion?"

"Your new pupil," the teacher said scornfully. "She's too good for us."

"I'm nothing of the kind," Annie said, "and I never said so. I just said I want to learn to read, not to play with yarn!" There was a measure of scorn in the old-young voice equal to that in the teacher's.

"Come with me, Annie," Mr. Anagnos said. "You may go back to your class, Miss Black."

He took Annie into his office and closed the door. Kindly he said, "You see, Annie Sullivan, you pose something of a problem for us here at Perkins. Not that it's your fault, but the fact remains that you know as little as the least of our pupils—and yet you are almost a young woman."

Annie didn't know why, but she felt herself blushing. She was silent.

"I just don't know quite what to do with you."

Annie leaned forward in her chair. "Just teach me to read, Mr. Anagnos. That's all you have to do. Just teach me to read."

VII. Friendships

Getting more grimy, more tired and more distraught each day of her long, slow train trip to Tuscumbia, Annie began to feel as if her mind were divorced from her body. This was the third day of her journey. She had changed trains four times and according to the conductor had two changes still ahead of her. But at long last, the end seemed to be in sight. If all went well, and if she missed neither of the two remaining connections, she should reach Tuscumbia this evening. She was very uncomfortable in her heavy woolen dress. She sighed, pushed the straggling hair off her forehead, and put on her dark glasses again. Her eyes burned, and her head ached.

She leaned her head back against the cushion, closed her eyes, and was again back at Perkins. It did not help her headache to think of how miserable she had been and how defiant in her misery. "Everything in my fourteen years had *un*trained me for fitting into the life at Perkins," she thought wryly. Deliberately, she pushed the unhappy memories to the back of her mind and called up a picture of Miss Moore.

The other teachers, it had seemed to Annie, had lined up in a solid front against her, but Miss Moore had somehow understood. There was the day, after she had learned to spell a bit—but badly—when her composition, over which she had worked long and hard, was read before the class. Her scalp prickled when Miss Jones said, "Now I am going to read Annie's composition aloud." She was proud of what she had written. When she had finished it the night before it was with a feeling of satisfaction. "Really, I know so much more than these other silly girls," she said to herself. "I have *ideas.*" Now apparently Miss Jones had recognized that fact and was about to proclaim it publicly. Annie sat up straighter and folded her hands on the desk before her. A little superior smile played over her lips.

"Annie has chosen to write," Miss Jones said, "on 'Silver Spoon Butler.'" Annie cocked her head. Did she detect a note of sarcasm in Miss Jones's tone as she pronounced the name? "He is an Irishman as you might guess." Here the girls tittered, and Annie felt her face flush. She steeled herself. The feeling of exultation which had flooded her a moment before already was ebbing away leaving doubt and fear in its wake.

"The composition begins thus," Miss Jones continued: "Mr. Ben Butler, who practally everyone knows as 'Silver Spoon Butler' . . ." She pronounced "who" and "practally" in an exaggerated manner and stopped before she came to the end of the sentence. "Our Annie has chosen to make free with the King's English in her weird spelling as well as in her incorrect grammar. 'Practally.' P-R-A-C-T-A-L-L-Y, practally," she spelled. The girls, who had begun to giggle on Miss Jones's remark about the King's English, burst now into open laughter.

Annie jumped up. "Laugh, you silly things! Laugh!" she shouted. "You haven't got any better sense."

"Annie," said Miss Jones sternly, "go and sit on the stairs till the end of the hour."

"I won't. I won't sit on the stairs! I'm tired of being treated like a baby!"

Instead of going to the stairs she had gone to her room and sat dejectedly staring out the window, though she could not see what lay beyond it. There was only one bright spot in her day—the hour she spent in Miss Moore's class. That class would come next. Would she be denied it? Probably.

A knock sounded on her door. She sighed. That would be Mr. Anagnos, and she knew from recent encounters with him that his patience with her was running thin.

"Come in," she said, the note of defiance, her badge of courage, back in her voice.

To her surprise it was not Mr. Anagnos who spoke, but Miss Moore.

"Annie," she said, her voice warm and friendly, "how would you like to bring your compositions to me privately when you have finished writing them, and I will try to help you with the grammar and spelling?"

"Oh, Miss Moore, *would* you? Would you *really?* I have good ideas to write about."

"If you would like to do that," Miss Moore said quietly, "you may come to me at nine o'clock any morning. I have no class at that hour."

"Thank you," Annie said, and the door closed, leaving her alone again. The class bell rang. Suddenly, exultantly, it came to Annie that she had not been refused entrance to Miss Moore's class next hour. Gleefully she grabbed her book and ran out. Miss Moore was her friend.

She realized now how much Miss Moore's friendship had meant to her during those first months and years at Perkins. It had made her realize her shortcomings; particularly it had made her aware of the futility of her lawlessness. It had gentled her from a wild thing into a human being. And Annie Sullivan, at twenty, en route to her first job, was grateful.

She was grateful, too, to Mrs. Hopkins, who had come into her life three years after Miss Moore had entered it. Since she chose to dwell on the pleasant things today, she drifted from thoughts of Miss Moore to thoughts of Mrs. Hopkins. She remembered the day Sophia Hopkins first arrived at Perkins. The summer before, Annie had undergone the most successful operation on her eyes to date. Young Dr. Bradford had performed the surgery at the Massachusetts Eye and Ear Infirmary in Boston just a year after his first attempt, and this time, with a year of treatments in between, Annie could see. She could not see well, but she could see.

So when Mrs. Hopkins arrived to be matron of the

cottage in which Annie lived, Annie actually saw her—
and she liked what she saw. Mrs. Hopkins had a strong
face. It made Annie think that she had stood up to life,
refusing to let it defeat her. A certain sadness in the gray
eyes indicated that she had known unhappiness, but she
showed no signs of depression. Her face held courage and
a serenity that Annie admired though she herself lacked
it. It was from Miss Moore that she learned what had
caused the look of sadness and why Mrs. Hopkins had
come to Perkins.

"She had a daughter," Miss Moore said, "about your
age, who died."

"When?" Annie asked, subdued, thinking of Jimmie.

"About the time you came here to Perkins. That left
Mrs. Hopkins alone."

"Doesn't she have a husband?"

Miss Moore shook her head. "He was a sea captain,
and he was lost at sea soon after they were married, even
before the daughter was born, I believe."

"So she's all alone?"

Miss Moore nodded. "And she wanted to do something that would be useful, and . . ." Miss Moore's eyes
softened. ". . . I am sure she has found the right place."

As time went on, Annie realized more and more that
this was true. Mrs. Hopkins was kind to all the sixteen
girls in her cottage, but she was also firm with them. To
Annie, who needed help so much, she gave unstintingly of
herself, but also she demanded much of her.

"You're a bright girl, Annie, and an attractive girl when you don't let your Irish temper run away with you or your stubborn pride put you on the defensive. I'd be the last to want to see your spirit broken, but I'd like to see it channeled where it will do some good. The only real happiness we find in this world is through what we do for others. Don't ever forget that, Annie."

Annie was not particularly surprised when Mr. Anagnos called her to his office one morning and said, "Annie, I've a class of ten-year-old girls who are supposed to be learning history, but for all they know or care Napoleon might have been a Roman god or a Greek patriarch."

Annie laughed.

"With your enthusiasm, perhaps you could take them over and generate a little interest."

"Mrs. Hopkins suggested this," Annie thought, but she didn't say it. She had learned to curb her tongue somewhat after those first miserable days at Perkins. Well, this just might prove to be fun. The idea appealed to her vanity, and the thought of having some authority was sweet.

"I can try," she said stanchly.

"Good girl!"

Mrs. Hopkins tried to find out about it that night after supper in the cottage. "Did anything interesting happen to you today, Annie?"

Annie's eyes twinkled mischievously. "Sure and isn't

everything that happens to ye interestin'? Haven't I heard ye say so with me own ears?"

Mrs. Hopkins knew she'd been caught. She laughed. "Did Mr. Anagnos call you in today? And don't answer me in that Irish brogue!"

"He did." Annie was in a teasing mood and chose to go no further.

"And what did he want?"

"As if ye didn't know!"

"But I don't know how you reacted to his suggestion."

"And you'd like to know?"

"I would."

For a moment Annie had thought to continue her teasing, but when she looked at Mrs. Hopkins' kind, hopeful face, she relented.

"Favorably enough," she said, "to agree to try."

That, Annie thought now, had been the beginning of her teaching career, and this job she had taken with the Kellers would be a continuation of it. She had liked teaching history to the younger girls at Perkins. She had dramatized it and made it come alive for them. "Let's each one take a new name this morning," she said one day. "We'll all be generals and kings!" The girls had liked her game. They liked Annie—especially the shy, lonely ones, for whom she had an especial tenderness. Before she was through with the class they had come to like history.

One of the biggest and nicest things Mrs. Hopkins

ever did for Annie that first year took place in June. It was the week before school was out for the summer. Annie had been testy and difficult for some time. She dreaded the summer months. When the other children went home, there was no place for Annie to go. The summer following her first year at Perkins she had gone home with another girl; this had not proved to be a happy solution. The next summer they had found her a job in a rooming house doing light work, but she did not care for her status as servant. Now another summer lay ahead, and as yet there was no solution to the problem of what to do with Annie Sullivan. She tossed unhappily in her bed at night. She was short with the other girls at breakfast. It was a Saturday, and there were no classes, but the students had their regular morning exercise period in the yard. As Annie was getting ready to go out with the rest, Mrs. Hopkins called her.

"Annie," she said, "I'll let you go in just a minute, but first I want to extend you an invitation."

"An invitation?" Annie asked ungraciously.

"Yes, I would like to have you spend the summer with me at my home on Cape Cod. I think you would enjoy the Cape."

"You think I—I . . ." Annie stuttered.

"Yes, I think you would enjoy the water."

"Oh, Mrs. Hopkins!" Annie had suddenly come alive. "Do you mean it? Do you really want me?"

"I really want you," Mrs. Hopkins said, smiling serenely. "Now you hurry along and catch up with the others."

To be really wanted, Annie had thought then, was the nicest thing that had ever happened to her.

She still thought so now as she gathered her belongings preparatory to getting off the train to make her next-to-last change before Tuscumbia. "I guess I'm really wanted now too. Captain Keller's letter certainly sounded as if they wanted me. I only hope this turns out as well as my summers with Mrs. Hopkins!" But at the moment she did not feel the rush of joy she had felt when Mrs. Hopkins had extended her invitation three years before. In fact, the nearer she came to Tuscumbia the greater grew her trepidation. "But remember, my girl," she told herself, "you need a job as badly now as you needed a place to stay then. And besides, perhaps you will be successful in reaching this blind and deaf child, and if you are, surely you will know some of that satisfaction which Mrs. Hopkins says comes from doing something for others. At any rate, you'll have the satisfaction of twenty-five dollars a month that's *your own money*." She tripped down the steps from the train to the brick platform below and nimbly dodged around a ladder which stood in her way.

"No use taking risks!" she laughed up at the porter who stood watching her and chuckling.

"That's right, Miss. Ain't no use takin' risks that ya don't have to."

"But then there are certain chances that you *do* have to take," Annie thought.

VIII. "Our Especial Place"

Annie didn't have to wait long for her next-to-last train. "I'm getting more and more dishevelled," she thought as she settled into another dirty green plush seat and threw her bonnet off. "By the time I arrive, I'll be no shakes of the well-dressed young lady from Boston that Mrs. Hopkins thought she was sending forth three days ago. Dear Mrs. Hopkins!"

The first summer at Cape Cod had been wonderful— and the second—and the third. With the thought now of the cool water lapping around her bare feet when she walked along the shore, she was almost overwhelmed with homesickness. Again she could feel the delicious coolness of the big house that belonged to Mrs. Hopkins' mother, whom she had soon learned to call Aunt Crockett. A smile curved her lips as she thought of the times she'd been allowed in the parlor to dust. In it were all Aunt Crockett's treasures brought back from distant lands by her husband, who also had been a sea captain. They became Annie's treasures too, which she carried close in her heart. Her favorites among them were the blue Delft dishes from Holland and the lovely china dolls on the mantlepiece, with their tiny baskets of fruits and flowers, beautiful in their perfection. Somehow it was the blue she remembered best—the blue of the Delft and the blue of the dolls' eyes. Always, even in those long-ago days in the cottage at Feeding Hills, she had longed for beautiful eyes, and always she had heard, "The child would be pretty if it wasn't for her eyes."

Feeling the gritty dirt from the train against her eyeballs, she removed her dark glasses and pressed her hand over her aching eyes. Even though she could see now, her eyes were still not pretty to look at, and often, as now, they hurt almost unbearably.

The scene in her mind shifted from Cape Cod to Perkins—to her last year. She was to graduate in June. There were four girls and four boys in the graduating class. The first of May the valedictorian would be announced. Annie Sullivan, appalled at her own ignorance and avid for learning when she had entered Perkins Institute six years before, had absorbed knowledge like a sponge. She herself knew that in all likelihood her grades would average higher than those of any of the other graduates, but she also knew that there were still great wastelands in her mind—areas which the Perkins curriculum did not touch.

It was with mixed feelings that she listened to Mr. Anagnos when he called her in to give her the news at the beginning of May.

"Annie," he said, "you probably know what I'm going to say." He shook his head. "When I think what a wild one you were when you came to us six years ago! There were times when I despaired."

Annie rolled her eyes and a mischievous grin spread over her face. "Sure an' ye thought ye had a new species for your scientists, didn't ye?"

He nodded. "Yes, but I still had faith in you and so did Miss Moore . . ."

"And Mrs. Hopkins . . . " Annie grew serious. She leaned forward in her chair. "I'll be forever grateful."

Mr. Anagnos reached out and took both her hands in his. "You've more than justified our faith, Annie. We're very proud of you. I'm sure you know why I called you in."

"I've an idea," Annie admitted, her mischievous smile flashing again.

"There was no question, but the grades of our eight graduates in the class of 1886 have been carefully averaged, and Annie Sullivan's average is at the top. I know you will do Perkins proud in your valedictory."

"Thank you, Mr. Anagnos. I'll do my best."

She rose to go, but as she turned toward the door Mr. Anagnos' hand closed on her shoulder. "You've grown into a very attractive young woman, Annie Sullivan," he said.

Annie threw her head back and in mock seriousness said, "Anne Mansfield Sullivan, Sir."

Mr. Anagnos laughed. "I'd noticed the addition of 'Mansfield' to your signature recently. Tell me, just where in the world did you get that particular name?"

Annie laughed too, and, putting a finger to her lips, said, "Don't tell; I got it out of my head. I tried several on for size but I thought this sounded the most aristocratic, so I've adopted it."

"I like you, Annie Mansfield Sullivan." Mr. Anagnos opened the door for her, and she went whistling down the corridor to find Mrs. Hopkins and tell her the good news.

From that time on the tempo of life at Perkins picked up for Annie like the vivace movement of a symphony.

"I'll make your dress," Mrs. Hopkins said. "We'll go into town and look for material on Saturday."

One evening before the day of the shopping expedition, Mr. Anagnos came to Annie and Mrs. Hopkins with a newspaper in his hand.

"Look at this," he said, pointing to a picture.

"Oh, it's that darling Frances Folsom who's going to be married to President Cleveland!" Annie exclaimed.

Everyone had been following with interest the news of the coming marriage on June 2 of young Miss Frances Folsom to the President. It would be the first time a President of the United States had ever been married in the White House.

Mr. Anagnos nodded and smiled and, turning to Mrs. Hopkins, said, "Do you see a resemblance to anyone we know, Mrs. Hopkins?"

Mrs. Hopkins looked at the picture for a moment.

Then her face, too, broke into a smile. "Why, of course!" she exclaimed. "Our Annie!"

"Isn't it remarkable!" Mr. Anagnos said. "Look at the shape of the head and face and the style of the hairdo."

Annie giggled. "It's just the pompadour. I don't really look like her."

"I think you're wrong," Mrs. Hopkins said, cocking her head and looking first at Annie then at the photograph. "There's a distinct resemblance."

Suddenly Mrs. Hopkins had an idea. "We'll make the most of this!" She continued, "I remember seeing a picture of Frances Folsom in her graduation dress when she was graduated from Wells. I'll hunt it up, and we'll copy your graduation dress from it!"

"Oh, Mrs. Hopkins, no!" Annie cried. But she was pleased, and knowing Mrs. Hopkins as she did, she hadn't a doubt that she would carry out her idea.

The shopping expedition was the thrill of Annie's young life.

"First we'll get the white muslin for your dress," Mrs. Hopkins said, "then we'll look for white shoes."

"White shoes!" Annie cried in an ecstasy of delight. This was beyond her fondest dreams.

Mrs. Hopkins nodded. "I've written my mother to send me some Valenciennes lace that's just packed away in a drawer at home with nobody getting any good out of it. You noticed the ruffles on Miss Folsom's dress were lined with lace?"

Annie nodded dumbly. She remembered every detail.

"And you shall have a pink sash. I asked my mother to send that too but it's only going to be a loan, Annie. It was Florence's. She wore it when she was graduated from high school. I would like you to wear it for your graduation from Perkins."

"Oh, Mrs. Hopkins!" Annie said in a hushed voice. She recognized the name of Mrs. Hopkins' daughter who had died. "Thank you."

"You're entirely welcome, my child, or I wouldn't be doing it."

The morning of June 10 dawned bright and lovely. Annie awakened when the first pink rays of dawn reached tentative fingers through her east window.

"Oh! This is the day!" she thought rapturously, linking her hands over her head and stretching deliciously.

The commencement exercises were to be held at Tremont Temple. The whole school went to the exercises— the pupils, teachers, and help, 180 strong—plus many invited guests. Annie herself had sent but one invitation, to Mr. Sanborn, to whom she felt she owed her admittance to Perkins.

She had received no reply. She thought about this now as she contemplated the day ahead. It was the one dark spot on her horizon. She *did* think Mr. Sanborn might have answered her note, even if he couldn't come. She had never seen her benefactor, and she had hoped on this joyous day to be able to do so.

Mrs. Hopkins had laid out her lovely dress on the bed, the pink sash beside it. The other girls in the cottage crowded around as Mrs. Hopkins did Annie's hair and helped her into the dress. When the dress had gone over her head and Mrs. Hopkins was hooking her up, she caught sight of herself in the mirror. "Why I *do* look like Frances Folsom!" she exclaimed.

"Of course you do. That's what we've been telling you," Mrs. Hopkins replied tranquilly.

"Of course you helped, making those little ringlets at my temples with your curling iron."

Mrs. Hopkins chuckled. "I believe you're as excited graduating as she was marrying the President."

Annie sighed. "I'm *more* excited, I'm sure. Dear Mrs. Hopkins! I do thank you. I can hardly believe it's me." She threw her arms around Mrs. Hopkins in a sudden, unwonted expression of affection.

Then they were at the Temple and Miss Moore was pinning a bunch of roses just the color of her sash at her waist. Annie gasped. "Oh, they're lovely!" It was all so wonderful—and she was so frightened that she suddenly felt faint. Mr. Anagnos had been standing by while Miss Moore pinned on the roses, and now he took her hand. "Time to go, Annie." His voice was warm.

He led her up the steps and to her seat on the platform. The exercises began. She saw it all as in a dream—Charles Prescott, another member of the graduating class, at the organ, his hands and feet moving rhythmically; Dr. Eliot, whom they all knew, as he was president of the Perkins Corporation and visited the Institute often; the Governor. There was music by the school band and by a double quartet of pupils who, Annie knew, were singing words composed by the late, young Mrs. Anagnos. There were the usual demonstrations by pupils of the institution—one in geography and one in early history of Boston, the latter done by means of clay modeling, musket drill, and dumb-bell exercises. Then there was more music.

Through it all Annie sat woodenly, hearing nothing, the color high in her cheeks. Before her was a sea of faces, none discernible from another, all adding up in her mind to a tremendous audience. Mr. Anagnos had said the Temple Auditorium held 2,500 people, and certainly every seat was full. How could she, ignorant little Annie Sullivan, ever stand up and face them, let alone stand up and speak to them?

The two boys who had played a cornet solo sat down. There was thunderous applause. The Governor arose, the room grew quiet, and Annie heard the fatal words: "We will now have the valedictory by Miss Anne Mansfield Sullivan."

Annie's heart stood still. She felt as if she were made of lead. She couldn't rise. Then she heard her name again! "Miss Anne Mansfield Sullivan." The Governor must have seen her plight. He had given her an extra moment to collect herself. She couldn't let him down. She couldn't let Mr. Anagnos down—and Mrs. Hopkins and Miss Moore. She couldn't let all those people down. She stood up, trembling from head to toe. Somehow she must walk to the center of the platform. She wondered how. She put one foot out tentatively, saw the toe of her white slipper, and it somehow gave her courage. She walked to the rostrum, summoning all the courage of her Irish ancestors, and faced the audience. The Governor began to clap, and the audience followed his example.

When the room had grown quiet again, Annie began: "Ladies and Gentlemen!" Once she had spoken the three words, the room began to steady before her eyes, and she continued without difficulty.

After a little, she found that she was almost enjoying herself, and before it seemed possible, she realized that she was approaching the end of her carefully rehearsed speech.

"Fellow graduates," she concluded, "duty bids us go forth into this life. Let us go cheerfully, hopefully, and earnestly, as suits ourselves to find our especial part. When we have found it, willingly and faithfully perform it; for every obstacle we overcome, every success we achieve tends to bring us nearer to God and to make life more as he would have it." She did a little curtsy in acknowledgment of the appreciative applause of the audience and went back to her seat.

Dr. Eliot then presented the diplomas to the candidates and Anne Mansfield Sullivan was a graduate of the Massachusetts School and Perkins Institute for the Blind.

Her words echoed back to her now—"to find our especial part." But what was Annie Sullivan's "especial part"?

IX. Strange Challenge

The uncertainty of the weeks that had followed commencement was very close to the foreground of Annie's mind, for it was still less than a year since her graduation.

The glow of the drama that had surrounded her before and during commencement fell away like a dropped cloak when the exercises were over and she was faced with the routine tasks of packing and getting ready to go to the Cape with Mrs. Hopkins. For the first time, her spirits did not soar in anticipation of the summer there. The problem of her future loomed too large.

"I thought selling books would be wonderful fun until Peggy Morris told me how awful it was," she said to Mrs. Hopkins as they cleaned out dresser drawers.

"Well, she speaks from experience."

"I know," Annie said disconsolately. "That's why it discouraged me. But I do have to do something to earn a living!"

"There's no rush about it, Annie," Mrs. Hopkins soothed. "After all, you need a vacation."

"And you are good enough to give it to me. But before September I have to find something."

"How's the packing coming along?" Miss Moore asked,

stopping at the door of Annie's room and peering in.

"Oh, the packing's all right . . ." Annie's voice trailed off.

"But you're not, eh? After-commencement blues, Annie," Miss Moore commented discerningly. "They're a common affliction. You'll live through them."

Annie left her packing and sat down on the bed beside Miss Moore. "You think I should go to Normal School and prepare to teach."

"That's right. You've already proved you can teach, and that takes a talent, Annie. Not everyone can do it, you know. And it's one of the best ways in the world to serve." A little twinkle came into her eyes. "If you meant what you said in your speech yesterday, that's what you want to do—be of service to your fellow man."

"I meant it," Annie said seriously. "But it takes money to go to Normal School."

"We will get the money if you decide you want to go."

Annie squeezed her hand. "You've all done enough for me already. It's time I made my own way in the world." She was silent for a moment. Then she said, "Anyway, I doubt that I could . . ." She stopped, fumbling for words. "I doubt that I could teach in the routine way—the way that's expected of teachers. I'd always be wanting to let the poor little children up out of their seats. I'd . . . Oh, it's such a false situation, a schoolroom. If I could teach from life . . ."

When she and Mrs. Hopkins reached the Cape, Annie

started taking long walks alone. She knew she wasn't good company. She was too moody. And besides, she had to think things out.

There was another possibility besides selling books or going to Normal School, one which she had not talked over with anyone. She was quite sure that if she wanted it that way, she could marry Mr. Anagnos. In fact, though he hadn't asked her in so many words, he had certainly planted the seed in her mind that had set her to thinking about it.

It was in this pondering, undecided state that one afternoon she was feeling particularly depressed. She had reached a point in her wanderings where a little-used path branched off into the thick marsh grass. She stopped and peered down it. Seized with a sudden spirit of adventure, she took a couple of steps along it. Then she stopped to listen. Her heart was beating hard under her light cotton dress. This was a path she had been warned not to take since her first visit at the Cape. "But that's silly," she said to herself now. "He wouldn't hurt me. He's never been known to hurt anybody."

An old hermit was said to live at the end of this path. She had often come upon the path before in her wanderings and had looked eagerly down it hoping to catch sight of this all-but-mythical old man who was supposed to be the only person who ever used it. But no glimpse of life had she ever seen.

She started to sing as she proceeded along the path,

thinking to warn the hermit of her approach. She didn't want to take him by surprise. Still nothing happened, and there was no sign of habitation anywhere until she came around a little bend. Then she stood back, stock still. On a plateau of yellow sand stood a little shack made of flattened tin cans and scraps of tar paper. It made her think of a crazy quilt. For a moment she stood staring, her hand at her throat. In front of the shack on a crude wooden bench sat a little old man, a long white beard reaching to his lap. "Rip Van Winkle," Annie whispered. She advanced on tiptoe until she stood directly in front of him. Obviously he was napping. With a certain amount of bravado, she cleared her throat. The old head came up, but the very blue eyes showed no sign of surprise.

For a moment the two stared at each other. Then Annie said, "I—I thought you might be lonely. I've come to call."

There was still no change of expression on the wrinkled, weathered face. "Ain't ye afraid?" he asked.

Annie smiled. "I was," she admitted, "when I started down the path, but I'm not any more."

"Well, I don't want no more company. I've got plenty company—better'n humans."

Annie had spoken truly. She was no longer afraid. This was just an old man who knew what he wanted from life and had the courage to take it. She admired his independence. She only wished she knew as surely what she wanted.

"Oh?" she asked brightly. "Who is your company that's not humans?"

"My friends 've got feathers."

"The seagulls!" Annie exclaimed, looking up to watch one that seemed to be standing still against the blue sky, its white wings spread gracefully. "I love them!" And with a sudden flash of intuition, "You feed them."

He nodded.

He looked at her for a minute then got up and stepped toward the water. He uttered a weird, haunting call, and the white birds began circling in. Several times he repeated the call; then he started back toward the hut and the gulls descended upon him. They lighted on his head, on his shoulders, on his outstretched hands. "Don't be in such an all-fired hurry," he reprimanded them. "Shame on you! They know I'm gonna feed 'em," he apologized to Annie.

She nodded her head. She was fascinated by the sight before her.

The old man went into the hut and came back out with a pail of scraps and began to feed the birds.

"Thank you for letting me watch," Annie breathed when it was over. "It was lovely. May I come again?"

"Ye was quiet," he said.

"Thank you. I must go now. But I'll be back another day."

She left joyously, the beautiful sight of the hundreds of silvery gulls wheeling away against the bright blue sky an indelible picture in her mind, and the old man, she felt, a new friend. Somehow the depression which had been weighting her down more and more had lifted, and she felt light and happy as she had not felt in a long time.

It was in this mood that she entered the kitchen where Mrs. Hopkins was starting to prepare supper. "There's a letter for you, Annie," she said, gesturing to the table where she had laid it.

"For me?" Annie said in surprise. She picked it up and looked quickly at the return address. "Why, it's from Mr. Anagnos!"

She took a kitchen knife and slit open the envelope. She saw that Mr. Anagnos' letter was obviously one on business and that there was another letter, addressed to him, enclosed. Quickly she scanned Mr. Anagnos' letter. An exclamation of surprise came from her lips, and she turned to Mrs. Hopkins.

"He—he says he's recommended me . . . Or I guess he has . . ."

Mrs. Hopkins looked up with interest. "A job?" she asked. "What kind?"

Annie turned again to the letter. "I don't rightly know," she said, her voice hushed. She held the letter out toward Mrs. Hopkins. "Read it," she said.

"Oh, my hands are all floury," Mrs. Hopkins pointed out. "You read it to me if you want to."

So Annie read the letter aloud:

Dear Annie,

Please read the enclosed letter carefully, and let me know at your earliest convenience whether you would be disposed to consider favorably an offer of a position in the family of Mr. Keller as governess of his little deaf-mute and blind daughter.

I have no other information about the standing and responsibility of the man save that contained in his own letters, but if you decide to be a candidate for the position it is an easy matter to write and ask for further particulars.

I remain, dear Annie, with kind remembrances to Mrs. Hopkins,

Sincerely your friend,
M. Anagnos

"Deaf, mute, and blind," she said in awe when she had finished.

"Another Laura Bridgman," Mrs. Hopkins commented, looking closely at Annie.

Annie stood staring out the window.

"Have you read the enclosure?" Mrs. Hopkins asked.

Annie shook her head. She sat down by the table and unfolded Mr. Keller's letter. She was silent for a long time, and at length, Mrs. Hopkins could contain her curiosity no longer. "Well, what does he say?"

"She's seven years old," Annie said, as if speaking from a dream. "She was stricken when she was nineteen months. Dr. Alexander Graham Bell . . ."

"Dr. Bell?" Mrs. Hopkins repeated the name.

"Yes, they've seen him, and he advised them to write Mr. Anagnos."

"And Mr. Anagnos has recommended you to try to do the job." There was awe in Mrs. Hopkins' voice.

There was awe too in the very posture of Annie's body as she sat by the table staring at the letters before her. "I couldn't. I never could . . ." she murmured.

Mrs. Hopkins wiped the flour from her hands and sat down opposite Annie. "It has been done," she said.

"Only once—by Dr. Howe." In Annie's mind was the picture of the middle-aged woman, still at Perkins, whom Dr. Samuel Gridley Howe had reached in her total darkness and silence forty years before. Annie often had gone to Laura Bridgman's room in the late afternoon to tell her about the happenings of the day, using the finger alphabet of the deaf to communicate with her. To this day it was considered a miracle that Dr. Howe had been able to teach this blind deaf-mute.

Annie's heart was beating harder than it had been in the afternoon when she had sighted the hermit's shack. How wonderful it would be to open the world to a child who had no contact with it except through touch! But who was she, Annie Sullivan, to think she could ever accomplish such a colossal task? Yet even now she almost knew that she would attempt it. She had been waiting for something, she knew not what. Was this it? She had told Miss Moore she did not believe she could ever teach in the conventional way, yet she wanted to teach. Certainly this would not mean teaching in the conventional way. More than anything else, she wanted to do something that would be of some real service. Surely, if she could succeed, here would be ample opportunity to serve. In that little "if," however, lay the whole question. Were the odds so great that it would be foolish to try? She didn't know. She only knew that she had been strangely challenged, that she felt vitally alive again for the first time since commencement. She got up and quietly folded the letters back into the envelope and stuffed them inside the open neck of her shirtwaist.

"I'll set the table," she said.

X. *Arrival at Tuscumbia*

It was late August when Annie had received Mr. Anagnos' letter. Mrs. Hopkins would be returning to Perkins the first of September. She had not questioned Annie as to what she was going to do, but a plan was taking shape in Annie's mind, and she was almost ready to discuss it with her friend. If she tried to do this stupendous task which Mr. Anagnos had suggested that she might try, she must first prepare herself as best she could. And the best—in fact, the only—preparation she could think of was to study Dr. Howe's reports on his work with Laura Bridgman. These, she knew, were all at Perkins. Dr. Howe had been the first Director of Perkins Institute, and it was there that he had done this phenomenal work.

"Mrs. Hopkins," Annie said one evening. "I've written Mr. Anagnos that I will try." She gave a long sigh. Mrs. Hopkins' eyes were bright, but she said nothing. "I will accept this position as governess to Helen Keller on the condition that I be given enough time—however much time it may take—to study the records of Dr. Howe's work with Laura Bridgman before I attempt the task. Even then, I have no idea whether I will be able to do anything for the poor child. But I surely will try."

"It's what I've been hoping you would decide," Mrs. Hopkins confessed, her voice warm with approval.

"I will study his methods and see what I make of them. And I will try. I have made up my mind." Annie's chin was up and her mouth set firm.

"If Mr. Anagnos hadn't thought you were the best prospect, he wouldn't have recommended you. Of course it's a colossal task, and there's no way of knowing until you try it whether you—or anyone else—can break through to this child. But it's been done once; so it is conceivable that it may be done again. I am proud of you, Annie, for making the decision you have made."

"Well, I have to eat!" Annie said, suddenly laughing and tossing her head as if to toss off the weight of the task before her.

It had been only a temporary shake off, of course. She had received Mr. Anagnos' approval of her plan and had returned to Perkins in September. For nearly six months she had pored diligently over Dr. Howe's reports, straining her eyes severely in the process. She made careful notes of the things she wanted to remember. She spent hours just thinking about some of the methods he had used and the results he had obtained. As she read and thought and studied the hope grew within her that she might be able to do, not only what Dr. Howe had done, but more. She had lived closely with Laura Bridgman for six years, and she knew the limitations of what Dr. Howe had been able to do for this woman. She had never been able to take her place in the world outside the Perkins Institute; she spent most of her time awaiting some girl— any girl—to recount the events of the school day.

Dr. Howe had taught her the language she knew, a word at a time, defining and making clear to her the meaning of each. Annie wondered if there might not be a better way, quicker and more effective in its results, whereby the relationship of words, one to another, might become clear to a blind deaf-mute. Well, it remained to be seen. She had at last gleaned all she could from Dr. Howe's careful notes. She must try her own wings.

So she had prepared to go to Tuscumbia, and now she was almost there.

It was six-thirty by the conductor's big silver watch when he came to tell Annie that they were nearing Tuscumbia. She dreaded the moment that she would get off the train and meet the child that was to be her charge. At the same time, she could hardly wait to see her.

"Sure an' I'm like a little fish that's bein' torn into two pieces by a couple of hungry gulls," she thought, remembering how she had seen two gulls in flight performing this very operation one day when she had been at the old hermit's hut on the Cape. "Cannibals, that's what they are," the old man had said, shaking his head. "I'd ruther they'd let me mash up the dead fish and mix 'em with cornmeal for their feed, but sometimes I reckon they jist like t' go their own wild way."

"Sometimes life likes to do the same thing to people," Annie thought. This wasn't the first time she had felt herself torn—nor would it be the last.

Now, her heart pounding, she gathered her belongings together, the big doll for Helen under her arm. As the train slowed to a creaking stop the conductor helped her down the steps. Eagerly she looked about her.

A sportily dressed youth about her own age came to her. "You wouldn't be Miss Annie Sullivan, would you?" he asked dryly.

"Sure an' I would," said Annie, still darting quick glances around the platform for a blind child.

"Wa-al, we've met every blasted train for three days. I must say I'm glad you're finally hyar."

Annie couldn't help smiling at his southern accent. It didn't sound much like Bostonian. "Where's Helen?" she asked eagerly.

"Home," he said, and she caught the note of disgust in his voice.

"I'm James Keller, her half-brother. And this lady hyar is Mrs. Keller, my father's—the captain's wife." He did a little mock, sweeping bow, but Annie curtsied in all seriousness.

The young woman to whom she was introduced didn't look much older than she herself. She was attractive and nicely dressed, but there was an air of wistful sadness about her that touched Annie's heart. "Who wouldn't be sad," she thought, "with her own child locked in darkness and silence." But what was this child like?

"I'm pleased t' meet ye, Ma'am. I'm sorry you've had to meet so many trains, but it couldn't be as many as I've been on. Why, I've changed trains *six* times since Boston. Three whole days it's taken me, and I know I'm a sight."

"Never mind. You're here; that's the important thing." If Mrs. Keller had qualms about the youthful, travel-worn stranger who had been secured to take such an intimate, vital role in the Keller household she gave no sign. "Take her bags to the surrey, James."

The mock bow again—this time with straw hat removed and swept low. "Ma'am."

"I thought maybe you'd bring Helen along," Annie said.

"No," Mrs. Keller replied, her voice muted, "we don't take Helen out."

"It's bad enough when people come in," James added.

Mrs. Keller paid him no heed. "She knows you're coming, though."

Annie looked up in surprise.

"That is, she knows something unusual is happening. I'd venture she'll be on the verandah waiting for us when we arrive."

The mile drive behind the spirited bays seemed long to Annie. It was difficult for her to curb her impatience.

"I brought her a doll," she said, "from the girls at Perkins. Laura Bridgman dressed it for her."

"Can she . . ." It seemed difficult for Mrs. Keller to

go on. "Can she . . . Can Laura Bridgman, I mean . . . Can she really talk and understand?"

"Oh, yes," Annie said, "using the finger language of the deaf, of course. I'll have to teach that to you and your husband—and James."

"Not me," James said ungraciously.

"Oh, but Helen can't . . ." Mrs. Keller began.

"No, I know, but we'll be ready when she *can*," Annie said with far more conviction than she felt.

Mrs. Keller seemed quite nervous. "I think I should warn you," she started hesitantly.

"If you don't mind," Annie interrupted, "I'd rather you wouldn't tell me anything about her. I'd rather come to know her and to make friends with her in my own way."

James guffawed. "I'd like to see anybody make friends with that wildcat!"

"James, please!" Mrs. Keller pleaded.

"Well, Miss Sullivan will soon see for herself," he said, turning in a lane. At the end of it Annie could see a house. It was not a Southern mansion, as she had thought it might be, but it was spacious, with large verandahs and pleasant old shade trees in the yard.

"Yes, there she is," Mrs. Keller said. Annie noticed that her hand fluttered to her throat.

Annie strained her eyes to see. There was certainly more than one person on the verandah to meet them; in fact, it looked like a crowd to her. As they drew near, a gray-haired man disengaged himself from the others and came down the steps to the carriage.

"Captain Keller, this is Annie Sullivan," said Mrs. Keller.

Annie acknowledged the introduction but was in too much of a hurry to meet Helen to note his dismay at her youth.

She saw a boy of thirteen or so on the verandah, and a younger girl. The girl was, of course, Helen. In an instant she knew relief. She had for some reason been expecting a fragile, unhealthy looking child—probably because Dr. Howe's description of Laura Bridgman had shown his pupil to be such.

The girl Annie saw was strong and active, though her staring eyes bespoke her blindness. She was ill-kempt, however, her hair tousled, her apron dirty, her shoestrings untied.

"Oh, Helen, I left you all cleaned up!" Mrs. Keller gasped in despair. Annie did not hear. She had eyes and ears for Helen only. She started toward the child with eagerness, her arms outstretched. According to her plan it would be her first concern to teach Helen to love her. This must come before anything else, so that the child would have confidence in her.

She did not know Helen, however. James, she realized in the next instant, did. The force with which Helen threw herself on Annie was certainly comparable to the strength of a wildcat. It would have knocked her off her

F. KREJEL

feet had not Captain Keller, following behind, caught her.

This was not all. When Annie attempted to embrace her Helen shoved her bodily away. Then she grabbed Annie's small hand satchel from her with more of this abandoned, remorseless strength.

"I'm sorry," Mrs. Keller breathed.

James pushed the door open. "Follow me, Miss Sullivan, before the contents of your satchel have been destroyed by the little beast." He carried her small trunk and preceded her up the stairs.

"It's locked," she said of her hand satchel.

When she entered the room which James indicated, Helen was already there before her. She sat on the floor beating Annie's satchel against the wall with a ferocity that was frightening.

James laughed. "She's discovered it's locked all right," he said.

Annie went to her. She tore the frenzied hands away from the satchel and opened it. Then she watched, fascinated, as the child dumped the contents on the floor and pawed vehemently through them.

"Have a good time, Miss Sullivan!" James said sarcastically and, Annie thought, with relish. He turned on his heel and left them alone.

Annie saw by the look of disappointment on Helen's face that she had expected to find candy in the satchel. Obviously other visitors had brought her sweets. So, actually, had Annie, but they were in the hand trunk which James had set just inside the door. She took Helen's hand and, leading her to the trunk, made her understand that there was candy there for her. She gave her just one piece, however, and when Helen wildly demanded more and Annie could see that she was on the verge of a tantrum, she tried something else.

She placed in her arms the doll she had brought for her and stood back to watch the results. Helen's hands went quietly over it. A pleased look came to her face, though she did not smile. Annie tapped Helen's chest with her finger to let her know it was hers; then a sudden thought came to her. Why not start now, this very instant? Taking Helen's hand again, she spelled into it d-o-l-l. Helen looked puzzled. Annie went through the same motions again, then took the doll, thinking to give Helen the opportunity to spell the word back into her hand.

She had not thought rightly, however. Instead of reaching for Annie's hand Helen threw herself at her in a rage, beating her with clenched fists and kicking her shins. Involuntarily, Annie yelled, "Ouch!" She put the doll on top of a high wardrobe, well out of reach of the demon with the flying appendages, and prepared to defend herself.

XI. Conflicts

In the days that followed, Annie succeeded in taming "the wildcat" sufficiently so that she was able to teach her to spell not only d-o-l-l back into her teacher's hand, but c-a-k-e as well, and a number of other words. It was obvious to Annie, however, that Helen was merely playing a game. There was no connection in her mind between the object which the word represented and the word.

"I'm accomplishing nothing until I can get her to make this connection," she thought with dejection. "The whole key to opening the world to her lies in language."

She was sure that Helen had a bright mind. Seldom did she have to spell a word into her hand a second time before Helen spelled it back correctly into Annie's. But how to get her to realize that words stood for the things in the world around her was one of Annie's biggest problems. There were other problems too. She had determined before her arrival that her first job was to get Helen to love and trust her. In this she had known no more success than in getting her to see that words were symbols. Helen would not let Annie embrace her. The only person that she allowed this privilege was her mother.

The third problem was as difficult as the other two.

The family, it was easily seen, had given in to Helen's every whim since the day of her affliction. The result was a completely undisciplined, self-willed "wildcat" who threw tantrums every time she was crossed and did absolutely as she pleased. Annie could understand a family's trying to compensate for a child's handicaps, but in this instance it had gotten entirely out of hand and was one of the things that was going to have to be dealt with as soon as possible. But how?

Annie was so discouraged with the magnitude of her threefold problem that she threw herself on her bed, held her aching head in her hands, and railed against Fate. "Oh, why does such a thing have to happen to a child in the first place? And what am *I* supposed to do against such odds? It's too cruel!" Before she knew it tears were streaming down her face, and her eyes and her head hurt worse than ever.

Annie Sullivan did not give up easily. The next morning she arose with the determination that she would have a showdown not only with Helen, but also with the Kellers over the matter of discipline. She bathed her inflamed eyes with cold water, dressed in a crisp shirt-waist and skirt, and went down to breakfast.

The showdown came sooner than she had anticipated.

She had been appalled at Helen's table manners from the first meal she had had with the family. She ate with her fingers, reached into the plates of the other members of the family with her hands and took whatever she wanted, generally making every meal a disgusting ordeal.

"I'd as soon eat with the pigs," James had said to Annie that first day.

"You will keep still, James!" Captain Keller thundered. But Annie couldn't help sympathizing with James.

"Good morning!" Annie said brightly, taking the place assigned to her. It was not next to Helen, who sat beside her mother, but across from her, beside Simpson, the younger boy. "Umm! Don't they look good?" she asked Simpson as Viney placed steaming plates of hot cakes before them.

Just as Annie was drenching the hot cakes with maple syrup, Helen, quick as a cat, stood up and reached across the table, grabbing the top cake, dripping with syrup, in her hand. The syrup left a sticky trail across the table as Helen crammed the cake into her mouth. This was the first time she had molested Annie's plate. Annie's eyes flashed. As quick as Helen herself, she was up and had grasped Helen's wrist. "You're not going to take food off *my* plate, my young friend," she said grimly. "You will eat off your own plate and eat with a spoon."

Mrs. Keller gasped. Captain Keller removed the napkin he had carefully tucked in at his neck and stood up.

"Miss Sullivan . . ." he began.

Annie caught the reprimand in his voice and cut him short. "You brought me here to teach Helen. The first thing she has to be taught is to act like a human being." She had breath to say no more, for it was all she could do to keep Helen's arms pinioned. In their struggle Helen fell off her chair to the floor, and Annie went down with her.

"Really, Miss Sullivan, I must . . ." Captain Keller protested.

"Leave us alone, please," Annie gasped, looking up briefly from her struggle. The others had risen from the table. Mrs. Keller, she saw, was crying. James was looking highly pleased. But Mr. Keller looked like a storm cloud. "Leave us alone," she gasped again, "please." Annie's eyes held Captain Keller's. Grimly he followed the others out.

In the second it had taken Annie to dispose of the rest of the family, Helen had managed to break away from her. Instantly and unerringly she went to Annie's plate and dived in with both hands. Annie slapped her hands with all her strength, knocking pancakes and syrup in all directions. Furious, syrupy fists struck out at her. One found its mark in the pit of her stomach, and she strove for breath.

The battle ceased as suddenly as it had begun. Helen had felt Simpson's chair and found him gone. Quickly she went the rest of the way around the table, discovering that everyone was gone save the two of them. Annie held her breath. "She's bewildered," she thought. "She doesn't know what to make of it. She'll blame me though, that's sure."

She braced herself for another attack, certain it would come. To her amazement it did not, nor did Helen at-

F. KREDEL

tempt to take more food from her plate. Instead, she sat down in her own chair and began to eat her breakfast, eating as usual with her fingers.

"Well," Annie said to herself, "I seem to have won that round. I'll try another." She stepped to Helen's side, picked up a spoon from the table, and put it in the sticky right fist. It went flying across the room and hit the opposite wall. Annie whistled. "I'm glad it didn't hit the mirror," she said aloud. She forced Helen from her chair, propelled her across the room, and bent her fingers around the handle of the spoon. Puffing and panting, she managed to keep one hand over Helen's fist so that she could not let the spoon fly again, and with her other arm and her knees, half dragged and half pushed the fighting little animal back to her chair. She put one knee across Helen's lap to hold her down, forced the hand holding the spoon, first down to the plate, then up to Helen's mouth. Over and over she did this. Each time Helen tried to break away from her she slapped her. At last she felt the legs under her relax. She loosened her hold on the hand with the spoon. It went down to the plate and up to Helen's mouth of its own accord. Annie smiled grimly. She released Helen completely and returned to her own chair to try to eat some of her cold breakfast. As long as Helen was eating she would at least make a pretense of doing the same.

She did not, however, take her eyes off her antagonist. When Helen had finished, she picked up her napkin from the table beside her plate and threw it on the floor. Annie's lips set. She jumped from her chair. Helen stomped on the napkin and darted to the door. But Annie had taken the precaution to lock it as soon as the last member of the family had gone. Finding it locked, Helen flew into another rage. She beat on it with her fists and kicked it so hard that Annie thought a heel of the stout shoes might actually go through a panel. Annie was in something of a rage herself by this time. Bodily she pulled the furious child from the door and dragged her back to where her napkin lay.

"It's a good thing," she thought, "that I'm bigger than she is. It's the only advantage I have. She has the strength of an ox."

Pushing Helen down with her own body, she made her pick up the napkin. Again she pushed her into her chair. For another hour the battle raged. At long last, however, with Annie's hands guiding Helen's, the napkin was folded and placed on the table beside Helen's plate.

Annie sighed with relief, patted Helen's head, and said, "Good girl!" Though she knew full well that the child could not hear a sound, she also knew that she was quick to catch another's mood. She would understand the approval.

Annie went to the door and unlocked it. Helen went running off.

Wearily, Annie climbed the stairs and threw herself on her bed. She was exhausted, and she was miserable. Certainly this physical battling had been no part of her plan to reach and teach Helen Keller, but somehow the child must be taught obedience, and at the moment at least, this seemed the only way. "But I don't want to break her spirit," she thought. "I want only to channel it. Oh, if I only knew what to do!"

Suddenly the tears came and she lay sobbing, her head buried in her pillow. After awhile, spent with her struggle and her weeping, she dozed.

A gentle tapping on her door awakened her. "Come in," she called. It was Mrs. Keller.

"Oh, my dear!" Mrs. Keller exclaimed, seeing her face swollen with her recent tears.

Annie sat up. She felt better now. "But, Mrs. Keller, she *did* eat her breakfast *with a spoon* and she folded her napkin."

Mrs. Keller sucked in her breath. "Oh, that's wonderful, Miss Annie! Let me tell the Captain. He . . ." she hesitated and Annie caught the change of tone. "He sent me to fetch you."

"I'll wash my face and be right down."

"And no doubt I'll get me come-uppance," she thought.

A few minutes later, she entered the parlor where Captain Keller was waiting for her. He stood beside the fireplace, his arm on the mantel. Mrs. Keller was seated in an arm chair facing him. Annie saw despair in the young mother's face. Her own head came up. Annie Sullivan could do battle with Captain Keller as well as with his daughter. However, his first words surprised her.

"Miss Sullivan," he said, "I am dismissing you. I hired you to be a governess of my daughter, not to disrupt the entire household."

Annie swallowed. Then suddenly all her Irish boiled up and over. Her eyes flashed fire. Though she knew the King's English well now and usually employed it, on occasions, for fun or from frustration, she lapsed into her childhood Irish brogue. "All right! Dismiss me if ye like yer household so well the way it is and don't want it 'disrupted' as ye call it. Disrupted? Sure and 'tis a shambles, a grand and glorious and gamboling shambles. Let yer wife die of a broken heart. Let yer sons hate ye and hate life and all the goodness in it because ye force this disgusting way of living down their gullets. Let Helen remain in that terrible and awful darkness that drives her to fury. Ah, no, *Captain* Keller—Mr. Keller—Sir . . . Ah, no, don't let anybody change the way *ye*'ve decreed, that *ye*'ve commanded yer household shall be!"

She had come close to him as she spoke. Now she turned on her heel and marched to the door, where she paused to say, "Goodbye, *Captain* Keller. And may yer sins of pride and egotism and bullheadedness destroy ye as they're already after destroyin' yer family." She turned. "Disruptin'," she sniffed, slammed the door behind her and ran up the stairs leaving Mrs. Keller wringing her hands and the Captain standing, open-mouthed, staring at the closed door.

XII. The Cottage

The instant Annie reached her room she started pulling things wildly from her dresser drawers and closet. Tears were streaming down her face. "So ye muffed it, Annie Sullivan!" she raged to herself. "Ye've not only lost your first job, but what is far worse ye've let this poor, imprisoned child down. Let her down? Sure and ye've just bargained to keep her locked in her prison for life. Who else are they going to find who'll try to do this fearsome job? I was a fool to think *I* could do it. But Helen— Helen—they'll probably put ye in an institution just as Captain Keller's precious relatives are always telling him he should. Shut ye away from the sunlight ye love!"

She sat on the bed among her clothes, held her head in her hands, and knew despair.

A gentle tap came on her door. This time, however, Mrs. Keller's face was full of relief, and her usually sad eyes were full of joy.

"Oh, Miss Annie," she said happily, "he's reconsidered." Then she saw Annie's face. "My dear, I'm sorry; I'm so very sorry."

Now Annie's head was up and fire flashed from her eyes. "Oh, *he's* reconsidered, has he? Well, that does not mean that *I* intend to reconsider. In fact I may not."

"Oh, please, Miss Annie! Just when you were beginning to have some success! Remember this morning?"

"Yes, I remember," said Annie bitterly.

"Think of my poor little Helen. If you leave us now, there's no hope."

"But we don't know that there's hope even if I should stay."

"I have faith in you."

"I'll have to think about it. If I stay . . . Things are no good this way."

"But you will consider it?"

"I'll think about it, I said."

The door closed softly. Annie did just what she said she would do. She thought. "If I stay, things are going to be different. I'll have to get some co-operation from the family. They'll have to help me discipline her instead of hindering."

She got up and started pacing back and forth the full length of her small room, her hands clasped behind her back. "If I could only have her to myself—away from the others. Like this morning. If they'd let me take her away." Her mind caught fire. Those would be her conditions, the conditions under which she would go on—that they let her take Helen away! It wouldn't be easy. Mrs. Keller, even though she had another baby now, could scarcely let Helen out of her sight for a moment. The Captain, with his stubborn pride, wasn't likely to take such a radical suggestion from the young upstart who had just defied him. But she would try.

The gentle tap at her door again. "Have you had time enough? Will you stay? The Captain would like to see you."

"I have *not* had time enough. Tell the Captain I will come to him some time before supper." This was going to be on her terms. She was tired of this attitude of the southern male that he was lord of all he surveyed and, in particular, womankind.

When Mrs. Keller had left she began putting her clothes back where they belonged, planning what she would say to the Captain, as she worked. Then she washed her face and combed her hair and put on a fresh shirt-waist.

When she confronted Captain Keller in his study she was outwardly composed, but inwardly she was trembling. If this didn't work; if she weren't able to pull it off . . .

"Come in, Miss Sullivan. Have a chair."

Annie would have preferred to stand, but she took the chair that was offered her.

"Mrs. Keller has told you that I have reconsidered. In view of your reputed success with Helen this morning —though I do not approve of your methods—I have decided to let you stay. We will try it a little longer and . . ."

"I beg your pardon, Captain Keller, for interrupting," Annie said. "And I beg your pardon for being rude to you this afternoon. But I have my conditions too, and I

110

will stay on only if you and Mrs. Keller agree to them."

She saw the Captain's start of surprise. He swallowed, but before he could speak, she continued, "I have decided that I can do nothing with Helen as long as the family is constantly interfering. I am convinced that I can do nothing for her until she learns first to obey me. I believe the only way I can reach even that first objective is to take her away with me some place where we can be alone."

"Take her away?" The Captain seemed to have lost some of his usual assurance. "But her mother . . ." he protested.

"I know," Annie said. "It will be hard, but I believe it is the only way."

"I don't believe she could bear it," the Captain said as though talking to himself.

For the first time, Annie felt her heart softening toward him. It was his gentle wife of whom he was thinking.

"In the long run, it would be best for her, too. The only salvation for her—for any of you," Annie said, speaking more softly, "is to break through to Helen by means of language. I haven't given up. She has a fine intelligence so that . . ."

"Do you think so?" Captain Keller interrupted.

"I'm sure of it."

For a moment they both sat, silent. Then Captain Keller suggested guardedly, "I wonder about the garden house."

A picture of the little house a quarter of a mile or so away flashed into Annie's mind. She had walked there several times with Helen. She had not been inside but from without it looked a dream cottage. There was a piazza in front, completely covered with vines, that made it look secluded yet infinitely inviting. Why wouldn't it do—if the others would only stay away?

"Yes," she breathed, "if you would leave me completely alone with her."

Captain Keller agreed to her terms. The garden house was cleaned and aired. Two days later Annie and Helen set out on their great adventure.

So that Helen would not know where they were going the bays were hitched to the surrey and Tom, one of the colored boys who often drove them, took the two for a long ride. Helen loved to ride but this drive had been unusually long. She was growing restless by the time they pulled up in front of the cottage. She jumped down gladly as Tom reached up to help her. Annie took her arm to guide her up the step and into the large, square room which was to be their living quarters for two weeks. On this time limit, the Captain had been adamant. "I will not ask her mother to be separated from her for more than two weeks," he said firmly, and Annie had not argued the point. She hoped and prayed that two weeks would be enough.

Now she watched Helen closely. A look of bewilderment crossed her face as she saw that they had not returned home. Instantly she began to explore. Her dolls, her little rocker, the small table at which she sat to string beads and to work with the yarns Annie had brought to Tuscumbia—all had been brought to the little house so that she would have familiar things about her. She felt them all, and Annie thought she could see something of relief in the child's face. Still, she was obviously puzzled. She sat down in her little chair and rocked hard, touching her cheek often, which was her sign for her mother. Annie almost held her breath.

Very shortly the little Negro boy who had been assigned to them for the two weeks brought their supper. There was a small table on the piazza, and Annie asked him to set their supper there. It was like eating deep in the woods, Annie thought, for the leafy bower of vines was so dense that she could not even see the garden beyond. Helen ate heartily, using the spoon which Annie placed in her hand—and doing so without contest. So far things were going well, but Annie scarcely dared to hope.

After supper they went back into the cottage, and while Helen undressed her dolls Annie took the time to enjoy the big room with its great fireplace and spacious bay window. The servants assigned to its preparation had done well. The wide floor boards were scrubbed clean, and colorful braided rugs had been placed in front of the fireplace and in front of the bed. This must serve as both sitting and bed room, as the small room beyond was to be used by the colored boy. A fire had been laid in the fireplace, but Annie decided they would wait until another, cooler night before lighting it. Blooming plants had been placed in the bay window.

For a little while Annie luxuriated in its pleasantness. "It's as if it were my own little home," she thought. She pulled herself up shortly. She was not here just to sit and enjoy herself. She was here to do a job, and no small job it was. She turned her attention to Helen. She had finished undressing her dolls and was surely feeling lost again, touching her cheek for her mother, her little face sad. Impulsively, Annie went to her and put her arms around her. She was pushed rudely away for her trouble. Annie sighed and indicated to Helen that it was time to get ready for bed. Docilely, Helen undressed. Annie also made preparations to retire.

Helen climbed readily enough into bed, but when she felt Annie come beside her, she rolled instantly onto the chilly floor. As quickly, Annie was out of bed and after her. There wasn't far for her to run, and Annie soon overtook her. But overtaking her and getting her back into bed were two different things. Helen kicked and screamed and clawed as Annie pinioned her. She got away again and started throwing everything within reach at Annie—her dolls, the plants in the window, books, and smaller pieces of furniture.

The battle raged for nearly two hours. Bodily, Annie would get the child back into bed, but the minute she attempted to get in beside her, the struggle started all over. Finally, she could begin to see signs that Helen was tiring. "As if *I* weren't!" she thought ruefully, panting for every breath.

This time, when she had dragged Helen to the bed and laid her on her side of it, Helen lay still, sobbing and hiccoughing, but unresisting. Annie pulled the covers over her. Helen turned with her face to the wall, lying on the very edge of the bed in final protest. She did not move, however, when Annie crawled in under the covers beside her.

Helen Keller was learning to obey Annie Sullivan.

XIII. "W-a-t-e-r"

The next morning Helen lightly put her hand to her mouth, her sign for "cake." Annie spelled "no." For the first time, the child's hand did not rebelliously wad tightly into a fist or broaden stiffly to slap. Instead, it fell quietly to her side.

Annie's heart was torn within her. She rejoiced at the progress she had apparently made—even though it might turn out to be merely temporary—but at the same time, she was miserable at the sight of the homesick little girl going back and forth to the door, touching her cheek for her mother.

"I'll teach her something new," Annie thought. "Maybe that will get her mind off her loneliness."

She had brought some yarn with her and a large wooden crochet hook. She indicated that she wished Helen to sit in the little rocker beside her. Meekly, Helen drew up her chair and sat quietly as Annie put the yarn into her hands. She felt the crochet hook which Annie held with interest; it was something new. Annie tied a knot in the yarn and started the stitch, Helen's hand following her every movement. After a moment, the child nodded her head eagerly. Annie put the yarn and hook into her hands.

It took only a moment of guiding the little fingers until Helen was able to do the stitch by herself.

"She's very bright!" Annie said to herself for the hundredth time. "If I could only get through to her the idea that words stand for things." She sighed. "I suppose I'm asking for too much too soon. After all, if she learns to obey me in these two weeks I should be satisfied."

She heard a slight sound at the open window and looked out. Captain Keller stood there, shaking his head, a look of humility and vast relief on his face.

"It's wonderful to see her so quiet, Miss Annie," he said. "Thank you. I'm sorry I didn't trust your judgment."

"We won't worry about that," Annie said. "If only this lasts . . ."

Almost to Annie's disbelief it did last.

Their two weeks were nearly over. Helen was a different child. She obeyed Annie without argument. She had changed from a wild, disheveled, insistent, and arbitrary little demon to a neat, well-behaved little girl.

Each morning they had a lesson. One morning Annie had an inspiration. "Percy!" she called to their little Negro boy. Percy came running. "You sit down here at the table with Helen this morning and do lessons with us." Percy grinned and pulled up a chair. Helen's hands had gone instantly to touch and recognize her companion, and she smiled when she saw that he was to do lessons with her.

"You see," Annie explained, "I'm teaching Helen the names of things. I spell the word into her hand and she spells it back into mine. This morning I want to teach her m-u-g and m-i-l-k." She had Helen's mug on the table and a pitcher of milk.

Helen seemed to be trying, but the lesson did not go as well as usual. It was not because Percy was there, for she laughed when he made mistakes and patted his head vigorously when he did well. She kept confusing the two new words; she continued touching the mug when she spelled m-i-l-k or pretending to pour when she spelled m-u-g.

"She just has no idea yet that words are symbols," Annie said aloud, shaking her head, "or that we use them to communicate." Percy looked at her, puzzled. "Never mind," she said to him. "You don't have to worry about such things. You're a normal child . . ." Her voice trailed off. "Take her out in the garden for a romp, Percy, won't you? I'll be along presently."

After the two children had run outside, Annie sat staring into space, the old battle raging in her mind. "It isn't fair!" She used to think the same thing about her own lack of sight and lack of family and lack of opportunity. Some of this had been remedied in her own case. Helen's, however, was more difficult. "But I won't give up," she thought. "I don't know how I'm going to teach her that language is the tool by which we communicate, but I certainly am going to keep trying."

The two weeks came to an end all too soon for Annie. She begged to be allowed to extend the time but Captain Keller was firm. "A bargain's a bargain," he said. "We agreed on two weeks, and it has been two weeks."

"I know," Annie sighed. "And it has been profitable. But I keep thinking that with a little more time . . ."

Captain Keller shook his head. "You've done wonders. We're more grateful than we can say. But her mother is very lonely and this other . . . You may never be able to teach her language, you know, Miss Sullivan. You may as well face it."

They went back to the big house and, with one exception, when Helen tried Annie out by throwing her napkin on the floor, Helen did not revert to her former behavior at table. Even that one time she did not make an issue of it—especially when she realized that the members of her family were not going to take her part.

Not only at a specific lesson time, but all day long Annie spelled words into Helen's hand. They spent much time outdoors, and as they gathered the eggs Annie would spell e-g-g into Helen's hand, or when they petted the velvet noses of the horses she would spell h-o-r-s-e. Still it remained only a game with Helen.

One day when it was very warm and Helen had been playing with her usual companions, the Negro children of the place, she took Annie's hand and led her toward the pump in the yard. "Wa-wa." This was one of the few sounds which Helen made that was understandable.

119

Mrs. Keller had explained to Annie that it was a baby word Helen had known and used before her illness and apparently she had remembered it.

Annie, too, was hot and tired, and the thought of a cold drink from the deep well was welcome. As usual, though, she remembered to try to make a lesson of this. As they walked toward the pump she spelled d-r-i-n-k into Helen's hand. Obediently, Helen spelled it back.

Annie began propelling the pump handle up and down. After a moment the silvery, ice-cold water came spurting from the spout. Helen held the big dipper under it until it was full and drank thirstily. When it was filled again she offered it to Annie. Annie patted her head in appreciation and drank deeply.

Then Helen indicated that she wanted Annie to pump some more. Annie again put her weight on the pump handle, thinking that Helen wanted another drink. This time, however, Helen put her hands and arms under the water to cool off. As the cold stream gushed over her hands, Annie was suddenly at her side, spelling w-a-t-e-r into her wet hand.

Helen jumped. Then she stood as if spellbound. Annie watched her with fast-beating heart. Suddenly a new light came into the little face. W-a-t-e-r Helen spelled eagerly into Annie's hand. Annie felt the excitement in the child's finger tips. She spelled it again and again. Annie was kneeling beside her. She could hardly contain her hap-

piness. "Yes, darling, yes!" she cried, crushing her in her arms and nodding her head vigorously.

Helen understood! She had learned that everything had a name.

She broke from Annie's embrace and threw herself bodily on the ground, patting the earth. Annie was instantly beside her spelling g-r-o-u-n-d into her hand. Helen darted to the pump. P-u-m-p, Annie spelled. Helen's excitement was mounting, and Annie could feel the tears streaming down her own face.

"She understands! She understands!" she cried.

There was a trellis nearby with a great shower of purple bougainvillaea dripping from it. Helen ran to it, pulling Annie imperatively with her. T-r-e-l-l-i-s, she spelled. Helen put her hand to the vine. V-i-n-e. The wonder of discovery was glowing in Helen's face and Annie could scarcely contain her joy.

"Let's go tell your mother," Annie said, touching Helen's cheek in her old sign language.

Instead of responding as Annie had expected, Helen stopped suddenly in her darting about and stood perfectly still.

Then she touched Annie.

With her heart full, Annie spelled into her hand, T-e-a-c-h-e-r.

XIV. In Keeping

It was just one month and two days after her arrival at Tuscumbia that Annie had witnessed the miracle of Helen's sudden comprehension of language. In the following week she had taught her little pupil literally hundreds of new words. Once Helen had understood that everything had a name she wanted to know the word for everything. All day long Annie was kept busy running here and there with her, spelling constantly into her hand.

Again the thought came to her that she would not be satisfied with attaining for this child only what Dr. Howe had attained for Laura Bridgman. She wanted to go further.

There was company at the Kellers', and this kept Annie busier than usual. Helen loved company and kept asking Annie the people's names and words for the things they were doing and the items they wore. It went on and on all day.

Among the guests was a little cousin, Louise Adams, who was about the age Helen had been when she had the severe illness which resulted in her blindness. She was an appealing little girl, and Annie and Helen liked to take her with them when they went about the place.

One afternoon the three of them were sitting on the grass under a spreading live oak in the side yard. "Come to Annie, Louise," Annie said, holding out her arms. The baby ran into them. "I wonder . . ." Annie mused. A few minutes later, Louise was standing beside Helen. Without putting out her arms that time, Annie said, "Come to Annie, Louise." Obediently, the child came to her.

"Hmm," Annie mused.

Thoughtfully, she took the children into the house. "Louise understands even though she isn't talking yet, doesn't she?" she remarked to Mrs. Keller and Mrs. Adams, whom she found in the big, cool dining room sewing.

"Of course," Mrs. Adams said. "Children always understand before they talk."

Mrs. Keller nodded.

"Do you have some scraps there that Helen could sew together to make a doll quilt?" Annie asked.

"Would these do?" Mrs. Keller suggested.

"Fine," replied Annie. With a few snips of the scissors she cut some pieces for Helen to piece together. When Helen was occupied, she said to Mrs. Keller, "I'm going to my room for awhile. If you don't mind, I'd like to have Helen stay down here."

"Do you have a headache, dear?" asked Mrs. Keller, sympathetically.

"No. No headache today, thank goodness," Annie said.

"I just want to do a little thinking about something."

The two women smiled at her, and she went to her room.

The heat was stifling but she was alone. She pulled off her outer garments and threw herself on the bed. She thought she was close to a discovery—something that would give her a method to use with Helen, something beyond Dr. Howe's method of teaching Laura Bridgman. She wanted to be alone to try to fit the pieces together.

It had started with her observation of Louise's mimicry. Seeing Annie spell into Helen's hand, she would make motions with her own small fingers in the palm of Helen's hand, making Helen laugh heartily. Seeing Captain Keller carrying a briefcase under his arm, she must have a small magazine to carry under hers. When she saw the Negro women sweeping the walks she picked up a leafy twig and started sweeping too. How does a natural child learn? In Louise Annie had the answer—by imitation.

That was the way a normal child learned to *do* things. Then didn't a normal child learn to speak in the same way? By imitating what others said? Long before he uttered his first word he understood what was being said.

Why wouldn't this work with Helen?

"Yes," Annie said aloud, her voice vibrant with excitement, "this may be the key. I'll talk into her hand as people talk into a baby's ears. In complete sentences."

She pulled her knees up under her chin and clasped her hands about them. Both her hands and her knees were wet with perspiration, but she did not notice this.

Her thoughts were racing. "Then after awhile, just as a baby begins to put words into sentences, I believe Helen will do it too.

"For the time being," she decided, "I'm not going to have any more set lesson periods. I'll just keep talking to her about the things we're doing and answering her questions."

The dinner bell clanged. She could scarcely believe that it was dinner time.

The next day was Saturday, and Captain Keller did not go to the office. Ordinarily Annie spent the hour before luncheon in the schoolroom with Helen, teaching her words for objects she arrayed on a small table. But, putting her new plan into operation today, she was romping in the orchard with Helen. "Miss Annie!" Captain Keller called.

"Yes, Captain Keller," she replied, going toward him.

"Why aren't you having lessons?" he demanded.

"I've decided to give up having regular lessons," she started to explain, but he cut her short.

"Of course you must have regular lessons! I was hoping that by now you would be extending the lesson periods so that this fall you might spend the entire morning in the school room."

"I do not agree with you, Captain Keller. I have decided that the best way to teach Helen is to let her run about freely and absorb knowledge about the things with which she comes in contact. I am talking to her in sentences now, and she is beginning to understand."

Captain Keller's mouth pursed. "Are you sure this isn't just your imagination?"

"Yes, I am sure!" Annie flared. "Would you like a demonstration?"

"That won't be necessary. I believe I know my own child."

"I doubt that you do," Annie retorted. She turned on her heel and left him.

She was seething. Why couldn't Captain Keller understand? Or was he just too stubborn to let himself see? He had been willing enough to admit that she had made progress with Helen during the two weeks they spent at the cottage. But this was a different kind of progress that he was now refusing to recognize. The other was a matter of behavior. This was a matter of training her mind.

She went back to her game with Helen but her heart was not in it. Captain Keller had the unhappy faculty of making her depressed because of his continual doubting. Why couldn't he have a little faith in her—a little faith in Helen?

As soon as she could she broke off their play and led Helen into the house. She went to her room and got out writing materials. As she often did when depressed, she turned to her friend, Mrs. Hopkins. She would write and tell her about her new approach with Helen.

Helen followed Annie to her room. As soon as she "saw" the writing materials she indicated that she wanted to write, too. Annie sighed. "How I wish you could write," she thought, putting paper and pencil on Helen's table before her. "I wonder if I ever will be able to teach you to read and write. But my job now is to teach you to understand through language and then how to use it—which your father doesn't think I can do."

She seated herself at her own desk, but the paper remained blank before her. Suddenly she had become afraid. Who was she—Annie Sullivan—with her spotty education and her background at Tewksbury Almshouse, to mold another's life? Yet wasn't that what she was trying to do? The thought appalled her. Molding a soul, as the children had molded animals and birds out of clay at Perkins. This was a human life she was proposing to fashion! What audacity!

She turned to look at the brown head bent intently over the table as Helen made marks on the paper before her the way she thought Annie did it.

A lump caught in Annie's throat. "If I don't do it," she thought, "it's—it's a human soul left, lost in darkness. I can't do *that*. Oh, Helen!"

She caught her own throbbing head in her hands. As was often the case with Annie Sullivan, there was a storm going on inside her which nearly tore her apart.

She felt Helen tugging at her sleeve. She had folded her "letter" and wanted an envelope in which to put it. As Annie handed her one she spelled carefully in her hand, "Here is an envelope for your letter." No, she couldn't stop trying.

With a sigh she turned to her own letter and began pouring her heart out to Mrs. Hopkins. Her pen raced. She did not notice when Helen left the room.

"If only I were better fitted for the great task!" she wrote. "I feel every day more and more inadequate. My mind is full of ideas but I cannot get them into working shape. You see, my mind is undisciplined, full of skips and jumps, and here and there a lot of things huddled together in dark corners."

She stopped writing and stared unseeing out the window. Instead of the activity that was actually there, she "saw" little Jimmie whimpering in the black Maria as it carried them to Tewksbury; Jimmie's white face in his board coffin; the old women in the ward; herself, rough, untutored, defiant, blind. She shook her head to clear it of the dark memories and went on with her letter.

"Oh, if only there were someone to help me! I need a teacher quite as much as Helen."

Again she paused. Then at last she put into words the thought that was haunting her: "I know that the education of this child will be the distinguishing event of my life, if I have the brains and perseverance to accomplish it."

Ah, but there was the rub! There *was* the "if!"

XV. Gifts

Christmas was in the air. "Christmas," thought Annie. "I have never had a Christmas in my life. Not one." Now, even though she was in the Southland where there was no snow and no crisp winter air—her only associations with the season except loneliness and despair— Annie was becoming very much aware of the Christmas spirit. It was beginning to permeate everything at the Keller's—even penetrating the darkness of Helen's world and the brusqueness of Annie's soul.

"What wonderful smells are coming from the kitchen!" Annie spelled into Helen's hand as they came in from outside.

"Cake. Smells good," Helen spelled in reply.

"And cookies. I'm sure I smell ginger cookies," Annie spelled.

"Go see," responded Helen, suiting action to words. Annie willingly followed.

"Now what you-all doin', snoopin', 'round here?" asked Mandy, the cook, rolling her eyes.

"I said, 'I smelled ginger cookies,' and Helen said, 'Go see,'" said Annie.

Mandy threw back her head and laughed. "Laws,

now, Miss Annie, the way you's teached that chile t' talk into your han', it's just a miracle. Why, she a diff'unt chile. Heah—heah's one fo' you an' one fo' Helen. They's gingah, all right."

"Mmm, thank you, Mandy. They melt in your mouth." As she handed Helen hers, she spelled into her hand, "You tell Mandy, 'Thank you,' too, Helen."

Helen grabbed Mandy's hand and touched the palm quickly and lightly with her fingers.

"Laws! That tickles!" Mandy said, squirming and laughing the more. "Was that 'thank you' she said with them chicken tracks?"

"I'm sure it was," Annie said.

"Jis' a miracle," Mandy repeated, hands on hips, shaking her head.

Annie, looking into Helen's radiant face, was inclined to agree. Helen had understood sentences and had come to use them, though often sketchily. "Isn't it wonderful the way she's blossomed in nine months?" she said.

Everyone could see it except Captain Keller. Perhaps it was that he *wouldn't,* rather than *couldn't,* Annie thought. She sighed. She did wish she could win him over to her side. It would make life easier for all of them.

"Tell me more about Christmas," Helen begged, skipping for very joy as they left the kitchen.

"Let's ask your mother," Annie replied. Mrs. Keller had been an apt pupil and had learned the finger alphabet quickly.

They found Mrs. Keller in the big dining room which served many purposes other than dining in the Keller household. She was sewing, but she laid her work down when Annie explained what Helen wanted. "I've not had much experience with Christmas meself, so I'm not the best one to tell her."

Mrs. Keller looked at her questioningly. Annie was twenty years old. What did she mean, she hadn't had much experience with Christmas? Suddenly Mrs. Keller realized that she knew very little about this vivacious Irish girl who had come into their lives nine months before. Why would she make a remark like that?

But Annie knew. How well she knew! As Mrs. Keller started talking into Helen's hand Annie sat with her own thoughts. Two past Christmases stood out for her, both for their bitter, little-girl memories.

The first was before she and Jimmie had been taken to Tewksbury; she was staying with Cousin Anastasia Sullivan. It was the first time she had ever heard of presents at Christmas, but from the whispering that went on she understood that in the living room were presents and that they were not for inspection. In fact, everyone was strictly forbidden to enter that room. Picking a time when the family had left her alone, Annie went in. She remembered nothing about the other presents, but she would never forget The Doll. It had golden curls and lovely blue eyes. Beautiful eyes such as Annie Sullivan longed passionately to have herself. Somehow she had convinced herself that the doll was for her. On Christmas Eve, however, the doll went to one of Anastasia's little girls. Something had died in Annie.

The second time it had been all her imagination also. Her imagination and her terrible longing. It was the winter after Jimmie had died. Her cot had been moved next to that of Meg Carroll—poor, patient, long-suffering Meg—who was the nearest thing to a saint on earth that Annie had ever known. Meg had told her the Christmas story. Wise men had brought gifts to a baby they didn't even know! Then surely they would bring at least one gift for her!

She spun a fine Christmas story all her own. She would go to sleep very early on Christmas Eve. A wise man in flowing robes, with a turban around his head, would slip into the ward and very gently, so as not to wake her, would place a gift under her pillow. Sometimes in her dreams the gift was a lovely dress; sometimes it was glasses through which she could see everything clearly; but most often it was a beautiful golden-haired, blue-eyed doll.

She had gone to bed aquiver with excitement. When she awakened early the next morning she reached eagerly under her pillow. She could feel nothing. Frantically she tore at the bedclothes. "Where is it?" she screamed. "Where is it?"

"Where is what, child?" Meg, awakened by her crying, asked.

"My present! My Christmas present!"
She was out of bed onto the cold floor.
She tore the bed apart.
There was nothing.

She was brought back to the present by Helen's tugging her arm. She was spelling into Annie's hand, and for once Annie had not "heard."

Annie was soon caught up in the bustle and preparations for Christmas at the Kellers', and since for the first time she had a little money to spend, she was enjoying her own small preparations. Too, she must help Helen, who was knitting or crocheting or sewing on something for every member of the household. Annie herself did not like to make things with her hands. It had taken her two years to complete an apron which she was required to make at Perkins. So now it took all the patience she could muster to guide Helen in her projects. "She's going to be much better at this kind of thing than I am. And it won't be long," she said.

Annie had given considerable thought to what she should give Mrs. Hopkins for Christmas. She had finally decided on having her picture taken. After she had sat for it she decided to order another copy. When she received the prints she was pleased. By taking a side view of her the photographer had happily avoided showing the inflamed and swollen condition of her eyes. The result was flattering. The picture showed a very attractive young woman, and Annie could not help knowing it. She decided to send the second print to Mr. Anagnos.

When Annie went downstairs on Christmas morning, the double doors to the parlor had been thrown open. She could see Helen sitting on the floor by the popcorn-and-cranberry-garlanded tree, a new doll in her arms. Obviously she felt Annie's approach for she turned a rapturous face in her direction. Annie's throat was full.

In her mind's eye she could see the blank, expressionless face of the child she had met just a few short months before; she could see the jerky, constant movements of the arms, the legs, the head; she could see anger and frustration manifesting themselves as doll after doll had been hurled to destruction. The contrast between that child and this was like the contrast between the blackness and fury of a severe thunderstorm and the quiet, glowing beauty which follows when the sun comes out. No finer Christmas present could anyone ever have than this.

This was not to be Annie's only gift, however. Helen jumped up, laying the precious new doll aside, to get the slippers she had knitted for her teacher. Shyly, Simpson presented his gift. Even James, though pretending to make his presentation mockingly, had something for her.

Much as she appreciated these tangible evidences of the young Kellers' regard for her, it was to Captain and

Mrs. Keller that her deepest gratitude reached out. When the gifts had all been exchanged and Helen was again on the floor playing happily with her new toys like any normal child, Mrs. Keller took Annie's hands in hers and said, her voice choked, "Miss Annie, I thank God for you every day, but I didn't fully realize until this morning what a blessing you have been to us. Look at her!"

Annie nodded. "It's because we can communicate now." Mrs. Keller could be no happier than she about Helen's progress—and about her own flash of insight which had led to it. If she had gone on trying to teach her word by word, she might have progressed no further than Laura Bridgman.

Mrs. Keller shook her head and turned away, unable to say more. To Annie's amazement, the Captain gripped her hands when Mrs. Keller released them. He looked deep into her eyes, and though she saw that there were tears in his eyes, he smiled at her. In that smile was an apology, a plea for forgiveness, and a thank-you that made up for all the grief he had given her.

It was Annie Sullivan's first real Christmas.

XVI. Cross Purposes

It was March. Annie had been in Tuscumbia nearly a year. She and Helen were in their tree house having a geography lesson. The tree house was one of their favorite haunts.

Simpson came riding his pony down the lane. "There's a letter for you, Miss Annie," he called.

Annie spelled the news into Helen's hand and prepared to go down for the letter, but Helen was before her. As Annie sat watching her scramble down she thought about the year behind and the years ahead. Helen had learned much in that short year since the world had opened up to her through communication. She was having regular lessons now. What lay in the years ahead, both for Helen and herself? With all the reading she did for Helen, her eyes were very bad again. Would she be able to continue this? If so, where would it lead? She had no life of her own. The young people of Tuscumbia did not consider Irish Annie Sullivan who worked for her living one of them in any sense. All she knew of the gay picnics and parties they had was what she read in Captain Keller's newspaper or what James told her. She was happy, of course, in her work with

Helen, but there was a strange restlessness within her which would not be stilled.

Helen was back with the letter.

"Oh! It's from Mr. Anagnos!" Annie spelled into Helen's hand.

It was with a glow of pleasure that she recognized the familiar handwriting. Mr. Anagnos had been pleased with her picture. He had written more often since Christmas and, Annie thought, with more warmth. Was her restlessness in any way related to Mr. Anagnos?

She tore open the envelope eagerly. "Oh!" she exclaimed again, this time aloud. Then she spelled into Helen's hand, "Mr. Anagnos is coming to see us."

Annie's excitement must have communicated itself to Helen for she clapped her hands in delight. "When?" she asked Annie.

"On Thursday."

Annie was calculating quickly. This was Monday. Perhaps she could even get a new shirtwaist made. She would ask James if they could borrow his boat one day. They could take a picnic down the river.

The three days flew by, and Annie's excitement mounted. James was to take her and Helen to the depot to meet Mr. Anagnos' train.

"Suppose he's had to change trains as many times as you did?" James said to Annie as they jogged down the lane behind the bays.

"Sure an' if he has he's a bigger fool than I think he

is," Annie said. "I'd like to shoot the man that sold me that ticket in Boston. Taking advantage of a poor, ignorant girl!"

"You're not so ignorant," James said.

"He's changed," Annie thought, glancing at him. "It's been good for the whole family—what's happened to Helen."

They were approaching the depot, and she heard the whistle of the train in the distance. She had no more time to think of the Kellers. Her heart was pounding. It had been a year since she and Mr. Anagnos had parted. Would they be strangers? Had she only imagined that he had thought of her as more than an ex-pupil?

The train ground to a halt and there he was, coming down the steps, just as she had remembered him—handsome, to Annie's way of thinking, with heavy, dark hair and bushy eyebrows, wide shoulders and narrow hips. He was Greek, and Annie had thought in her late teens at Perkins, a Greek god.

"Annie!" he said, gripping both her hands in his.

Yes, there was a slight difference, Annie saw now on closer inspection. His black hair was beginning to show gray at the temples. "How old is he?" she wondered. Helen was at their side, demanding attention. Annie put the child's hand into the man's, spelling as she did so. "This is Mr. Anagnos, Helen, whom I've told you so much about."

Annie and Mr. Anagnos did not have a great deal of

time alone in the two days he spent in Tuscumbia. He had come to visit "them," and besides, Helen was so used to having her teacher's undivided attention that it was difficult to break the pattern even briefly. Of course, Mr. Anagnos, whose life's work was with the blind, was extremely interested in the progress Annie had made with Helen. "It's marvelous, absolutely marvelous!" he said over and over. "You've already gone far beyond what Dr. Howe was able to do. But I think you have a child prodigy to work with."

Annie bristled at this.

"Helen is bright; she has a quick mind. But I won't have her made into 'a prodigy.' I thought some of the things you said in the newspaper interview that Mrs. Hopkins sent me were ridiculous. She is just a normal little girl, Mr. Anagnos, who was shut off from normal intercourse for nearly six years. As soon as she learned the trick of communicating through sentences she's tried to catch up. That's all."

She could see Mr. Anagnos was not convinced. She smiled a bit wryly. She thought she understood. Mr. Anagnos wanted it this way. He could not admit that this slip of an Irish lass from the almshouse could surpass the great Dr. Howe.

It was James Keller who saw to it that Annie and Mr. Anagnos had the last afternoon alone together. The day before Annie had asked the loan of his boat. Teasingly he had answered, "Sure an' ye know ye may have it, Miss Annie, if ye'll be after takin' me along."

To Annie's disgust, she felt herself blushing. "Of course you can come along if you like. I thought we'd take a picnic down river. Helen loves outings and . . ."

Here James interrupted. "You're not taking *her?*" he asked, no longer joking.

"I had thought to," Annie said.

"That's not necessary," James told her. "Ill take her for a ride tomorrow afternoon, myself."

"That's very kind of you, James," Annie said, her voice softening.

So it was that when the picnic party set out it was a party of two.

It was a lovely day; the sky was a sapphire blue dotted with puffs of white cumulus clouds. "They make me think of the cotton bolls when they have burst open," Annie said, lying back in the boat as they drifted lazily down river. Her destination was "Keller's Landing," a picturesque spot that had been used during the Civil War to land troops, but now, unused, was overgrown with moss and tall grasses. The quiet and the solitude of the place always set her to dreaming. She had wanted to share it with Mr. Anagnos even when she had thought they were to have company.

"And that child you are training makes me think of the cotton boll when it has burst open," Mr. Anagnos replied. "It's as if an internal explosion had taken place. But you mustn't work too hard, Annie."

"It isn't work," Annie said, "and yet sometimes I do find myself exhausted. We almost never stop, you see."

"So I notice," Mr. Anagnos put in.

"Here we are," Annie said, glad for an opportunity to change the subject.

"Quite a romantic spot," Mr. Anagnos commented, helping her out of the boat.

Again Annie was annoyed to feel herself blushing. "I often bring Helen out here," she said briskly. "There's a spring of icy water over there . . ." He kept her hand in his as she led him around toward the small spring.

"It's a wonderful thing that you've done, Annie Sullivan. But what about you?"

They had reached the spring. "Well, what—what about me?" Annie stuttered. "Don't you want a drink of water from our hidden spring?"

Mr. Anagnos leaned and drank. "Mmm," he said. "Delicious." Then he dropped onto the lush grass beside the spring and pulled Annie down beside him. He was not to be diverted. "When I suggested you to Captain Keller for this position, I did it for two reasons. Because you wanted a job and because you were the only person I could think of who had the brains and imagination and stamina to tackle such a job with some possibility of success."

"I think it's mostly been just plain cussed persistence," Annie said.

"But there were other plans I'd thought about for you, too."

This time Annie did not interrupt.

"And I've thought more and more about them as the months have gone by. It's been a year, Anne Mansfield Sullivan, and I've missed you very much."

"I've missed—Perkins, too," Annie murmured.

"Just Perkins?" Mr. Anagnos asked. "You haven't missed me?"

Annie smiled. "Sure an' you're a part of Perkins, now, aren't ye? I thought ye were a very *big* part!"

Mr. Anagnos ignored her teasing. "It made me a very happy man when you sent me your picture. I look at it every day and wish you were there in its place."

Annie chewed a blade of grass and would not look up.

"Annie, I'm lonely," he went on, "and I can't think of anybody I'd rather have keep me company than . . ."

Suddenly Annie jumped up. She clasped her hands behind her back and started pacing to and fro. "Mr. Anagnos," she said, and stopped. This was what she had thought she wanted to hear, but now that he had started to speak, she knew that she must stop him. She tried again. "You see, Mr. Anagnos . . . well, I thank ye. That I do. And I must admit I'm often lonely meself. But . . . well, it was more than a job ye sent me to. It's more like a—a religion; it's something ye become dedicated to." She was talking rapidly now, gesturing with animation, and slipping into her Irish brogue as she

143

sometimes did in moments of stress. "I don't know how far I can go with Helen's education. Goodness knows I'm aware of me own limitations. But I've made a start with her and it's like seeing heaven open up before ye to see that child's mind unfold. What I'm trying to say, Mr. Anagnos, is that it looks as though when ye sent me here, ye were kind of a tool of Destiny. And I don't think that for our own little human desires, we've got any right to fool with Destiny. I have a feeling that my destiny lies with Helen—or hers with me— and I only hope . . ." Her voice became hushed. "I only hope that somehow I will know the answers when I need them—as I knew the answer for you today."

XVII. Perkins Revisited

Despite Annie's words to Mr. Anagnos on the final afternoon of his visit, before he left Tuscumbia he invited Annie and Helen to come to Perkins. "I don't know how to take the man," Annie said to herself. "Didn't he understand what I was trying to say?" Still, he had not pursued the subject of A. Sullivan and M. Anagnos further. Was he just inviting them so that Helen might have the advantages of Perkins Institute? Or perhaps—a new idea suddenly came to Annie and her eyes narrowed. Did he think Helen's presence at Perkins would be good publicity for his institution? She would not like to think so. Or did he believe that if Annie were near him for a time she might change her mind? "Perhaps he doesn't know why he did it; perhaps his motives are all mixed up, as mine are sometimes," she thought.

At any rate, whatever the reasoning back of it, he had issued the invitation. They had all been sitting in the parlor that last evening prior to his early departure the next morning when he had put the question. "Captain Keller, Sir, what would you think about Miss Sullivan's bringing Helen to Boston for a visit this spring?

We would be happy to have them at Perkins Institute."

Captain Keller looked at him with sharp eyes. "It's kind of you," he said.

"I have several business stops to make before I get back to Boston, but I should be there by the first of May. Any time after that . . ."

"Thank you very much," Captain Keller said. "Mrs. Keller and I will talk it over."

Mr. Anagnos did not press it. He said simply, "It would give Helen an opportunity to talk with other children who use the finger alphabet."

Captain Keller nodded and repeated, "Mrs. Keller and I will talk it over."

After Mr. Anagnos was gone, Annie couldn't help thinking about his invitation. Perkins was home to her. Mrs. Hopkins was there. Truly, it would be wonderful to go back! Of course there was the consideration of Mr. Anagnos' presence. Well, she had heard no more about it, so probably Captain Keller was not thinking of sending them.

One day, however, he called Annie to his study. "I have just had a letter from Mr. Anagnos," he said. "It seems that he is still thinking about you and Helen paying a visit to Perkins. He has a further suggestion here—that Mrs. Keller come also."

Annie brightened. She thought this was a happy suggestion and might be just the thing that would turn the trick with Captain Keller.

"I have talked the matter over with Mrs. Keller, and we think that it might be advantageous for Helen to have this association with other children who—who speak the same language. What do you think?"

"I have thought all along that it would be a very good thing for Helen," Annie replied instantly.

"Then we shall make plans for the three of you to go."

The house began to buzz from that moment on. There was sewing to be done; there were purchases to be made and a thousand small details to be attended to so that Mrs. Keller might leave Mildred and the house and servants. Helen was in such a frenzy of excitement at the thought of the trip that she was about to wear Annie out. "And I guess I'm a bit excited myself," Annie had to admit. It was near the end of May before their preparations were complete, and by that time several things had happened to make the trip even more exciting.

"Certainly Mr. Anagnos must have spread the news of our coming," Annie said in wonder when they received a letter from Dr. Alexander Graham Bell in Washington asking if they would stop over to see him en route to Boston.

"We'll have to stop," Mrs. Keller said, her eyes shining. "In a manner of speaking, it was Dr. Bell who was responsible for sending you to us."

Annie smiled. She had heard the story often enough to know it in every detail, but Mrs. Keller would tell it again. Indeed, it was the story of all stories dearest to her heart.

"We'd taken Helen to this Dr. Chisholm Captain Keller had heard about in Baltimore, but like all the rest, he said he could do nothing for her. We were in despair. But he said, 'I suggest you consult Dr. Alexander Graham Bell in Washington in regard to her education. He is much interested in the blind and will be able to suggest teachers and schools.' Dr. Bell was a very famous man. Everybody knew about him because of his invention of the telephone. But Captain Keller never hesitated. We went straight into Washington and went to see him, all three of us. He was so good to Helen! He held her on his knee, and he understood her signs. But best of all, of course, he gave us the address of Perkins Institute and suggested that we write Mr. Anagnos."

"And you did, and here I am," Annie said, "as big as life and lots ornerier!"

Mrs. Keller smiled at her.

Captain Keller wrote Dr. Bell that Annie and Helen and Mrs. Keller would stop to see him.

A few days later came an even greater surprise— another invitation—and this one held a very special appeal for Annie.

"Oh, no! I can't believe it!" she cried after she and Helen were called in from outside to hear the news.

Captain Keller, chuckling, held out the letter to her. It was from Washington, D. C., again, but this time the

148

letter was on White House stationery. It was from the President of the United States!

Annie read it with mixed emotions. What a wonderful opportunity! Meeting President Cleveland! Perhaps —she had to admit that this gave her an even greater thrill—they would get to meet Mrs. Cleveland, Frances Folsom Cleveland whom she was supposed to resemble! A gnawing apprehension was doing war with her pleasure, however. Was this going to be good for Helen? Already she had felt that Helen was getting too much publicity in the press. Yet Helen did not know about this clamor. Being presented to the President was something else again.

She did not, however, give voice to her qualms. Helen was the Kellers' daughter, and Annie would not interfere unless or until she saw real danger.

Their visit with Dr. Bell was all Annie could have hoped for, and more. He was delighted with Helen's progress and could not praise Annie highly enough.

"It's the best piece of work I've ever known to be done with a blind deaf-mute," he said, looking long at Annie. "And you've been with her only about a year?"

"A year and three months, sir. But Helen is a bright child."

"Yes, but it was you who turned the key to unlock her mind. It had not happened in the five years before they found you. I well remember the child's condition when they first brought her to me. I should be very interested to know, Miss Sullivan, everything you can tell me about the methods you have used."

"I'll be glad to tell you anything I can, Dr. Bell, but it's been very simple, what I've done."

He did not agree with this and insisted on taking her to dinner that night so that they might talk. When he left her at her hotel she felt more of a person than she had ever felt before in her life. The great Dr. Alexander Graham Bell had been unstinting in his praise. "He didn't even hint that the reason I'm being more successful with Helen than Dr. Howe was with Laura Bridgman is because Helen is a 'prodigy,' " she thought happily. "He just said right out that I had hit upon the right method and that it was wonderful I'd thought of it."

He had said something else which had not made Annie so happy. "You are doing a wonderful work, Miss Sullivan," he had said, leaning across the table and looking into her eyes, "but I am afraid you are dooming your own sight in the process."

"Oh, me eyes've always been the bane of me existence," she said, trying to pass it off lightly.

He would not let her brush him off.

"Even if you refuse to think of yourself, think of Helen," he said. It was something of which she had thought often. What would become of Helen if she should again totally lose her sight? She always pushed the thought to the back of her mind.

"I strongly urge you to see your doctor while you

are in Boston." Dr. Bell had not missed the fact that Annie had to press her face very close to the menu to read it. "And save your eyes as much as you possibly can."

Though the meeting with Dr. Bell had exceeded Annie's expectations, she was disappointed in a sense with their visit to the President. Mrs. Cleveland, the President said, would be sorry to miss them, but she was out of the city at the time. Annie hadn't realized until then how much she had counted on seeing Frances Folsom Cleveland. Nevertheless, she was thrilled with being at the White House. After a brief chat with his visitors, the President was kind enough to have them shown through several of the downstairs rooms. "It's the most elegant house I was ever in," Annie said in awe to Mrs. Keller as they went back to their waiting carriage. "But then I guess nobody has a better right to a nice house than our President."

Mrs. Keller smiled. Sometimes Annie seemed so naïve —for all her wisdom in dealing with Helen.

Just as Annie had expected, the actual return to Perkins was a true homecoming for her. To her delight, it was obvious almost at once that this was a wonderful experience for Helen. "She just naturally *loves* people," she said to Mrs. Keller and Mrs. Hopkins one evening. "And to be able to romp and play with these children that she can *talk* to at the same time is a great treat for her."

She did not, however, in front of Mrs. Keller, express

a conviction that grew stronger within her each day they stayed at Perkins—Helen was not ready for a formal education. They tried putting her in classes with the children her own age—"just to visit," as Mr. Anagnos expressed it—but she could not sit still. They tried letting her visit mornings only and rest in the afternoons, but while she was very interested in all the equipment—the modeling clay, the typewriters, the materials they used—she was not interested in the lessons as they were presented in the schoolroom. Annie could see that she was growing increasingly nervous.

"I'm not going to send her to any more classes," she said one night to Mrs. Hopkins when the two of them were alone. "She just isn't ready."

Not even to Mrs. Hopkins did she voice the question in her own mind: "I wonder if she ever will be ready for a formal education?"

XVIII. Conflict at Commencement

Time went by swiftly for Annie in her old environs. When school was out at Perkins she and Helen and Mrs. Keller went home with Mrs. Hopkins for the summer. The Cape was as lovely as ever, and to find the old hermit still there, feeding the gulls, gave Annie a satisfying feeling of continuity.

At summer's end, the three returned to Tuscumbia.

"Helen learns so much better in this unrestricted atmosphere," Annie sighed one evening.

Captain Keller looked at her over his paper. "But don't you think, Miss Annie, that sooner or later she should have the discipline of a regular classroom?"

"I—I don't know," Annie said slowly. It was a problem she herself had pondered often. It was not, however, so much the discipline of the schoolroom which concerned her as a question in regard to her own ability to give Helen the kind of education she should have and of which she was capable of absorbing. "I am trying to give her regular lessons in all the subjects the children her age at Perkins are studying," she said defensively.

Captain Keller nodded and went back to his paper.

Another winter went by. Helen learned to read and

write Braille, but Annie overtaxed her eyes to the point where she could neither read nor write.

"Teacher has a headache again," Helen spelled into her mother's hand when she came down to breakfast one morning in early spring. "She can't get up."

Kate Keller looked at her husband in concern. This was the third successive day Annie had lain prostrate. This had been happening more and more often of late.

"If you will excuse me, please, I'll go to her."

Kate Keller loved Annie Sullivan as a friend, and her concern was for her as an individual as well as in the capacity of Helen's teacher.

"My dear," she said, putting her cool hand gently on Annie's head, "something is going to have to be done for you. We can't let this go on any longer."

Annie sighed. "I'm afraid you're right. It isn't just my head; it makes me sick all over, and I'm no good to Helen or anyone else."

"And it *is* from your eyes; I don't believe there's any doubt of it."

There was a slight affirmative movement of Annie's head on the pillow.

"Dr. Bradford warned me years ago that . . ."

"He's the doctor in South Boston?"

"Yes, who—who gave me back my sight."

"I'll talk to Captain Keller, Annie. I think you should go back to Dr. Bradford. What did he say, dear? You said he 'warned you.' "

"That if I used my eyes too much, they would give out again—completely." She barely whispered the last word and Kate Keller saw the shudder that accompanied it. There was a lump in her own throat and real fear in her heart but she tried to disguise it.

"We'll manage somehow. You just lie quiet and don't worry. Here's a cool, damp cloth to put over your eyes."

Mrs. Keller went directly to her husband's study.

"We have to get her back to Boston to her doctor. Quickly. If it isn't too late already. Why, the poor girl can scarcely see at all."

"What about Helen?" asked Captain Keller.

"I don't know. But if Annie Sullivan is to be Helen's eyes, she is going to have to have her own eyes to see with." She shook her head sadly. "She's done this for Helen knowing that it might mean her own sight."

"Knowing?"

"Yes, she had been warned against overusing her eyes. She paid no attention to the warning."

"I'll make arrangements at once. And I'll get in touch with Mr. Anagnos to see if he can find us a substitute while she is gone. It might be . . . be quite awhile."

Mrs. Keller nodded solemnly.

It was quite awhile. It was more than four months, months in which Annie was torn between anxiety and loneliness for Helen on the one hand, and relief from pain and the luxury of convalescence on the other. There were days when she was as restless as a panther, and then there were days when she was as contented as a cat.

It was September before she was back in Tuscumbia, but she could see, and the blinding headaches which had become unbearable the spring before had subsided.

"You have learned your lesson? You *will* take care?" Dr. Bradford asked before dismissing her.

"I hope I've learned my lesson," Annie said mischievously, "but sometimes I wonder if the Irish *ever* learn. They're ferever tryin' to run on their luck."

"Well, I'm warning you, Annie Sullivan, the next time your luck might run out. I think you've pushed it to the limit."

Annie sobered. "I'll be careful. Truly I will. And I am grateful."

She had been back less than a month when another invitation came from Mr. Anagnos for her to bring Helen to Perkins, this time for the entire school year. He, himself, would be abroad, he said.

Captain Keller did not hesitate to accept the invitation.

"And this time," Annie thought, "perhaps Helen will be ready for regular schooling. She is going on ten."

So she entered her in a full schedule of classes, attending with her to spell into her hand what the teachers were saying. Helen not only absorbed everything that was offered to her but asked constantly for more. "Her questions are fit to run you ragged," Annie said to Mrs. Hopkins one night. "I no more than get the business of birth and life explained to her than she starts pestering me about death and heaven." She sighed. "An' that's too much for the likes of me. Do you know what I think I'll do?"

Mrs. Hopkins shook her head.

"I've read a good deal of what Dr. Phillips Brooks has written. He seems to be a very sensible man of divinity. I think I shall see if he would be willing to see Helen . . . . And let *him* try to answer some of her questions." She smiled impishly.

"You seem to think some of her questions might stump even the great Dr. Brooks."

"They just might."

Annie was very much pleased, however, with their interview with Dr. Brooks. She felt she had made a good choice.

"He makes sense," she said to Mrs. Hopkins the night after their return.

"Helen seems highly excited," Mrs. Hopkins commented.

"She's much more excitable here than at home. I don't know. I just don't know."

She continued to wonder as the year went on. Helen was making amazing progress, but she was also becoming increasingly nervous. Annie took wild, early morning horseback rides, alone this year in the absence of Mr. Anagnos. Her thoughts ran as fast as her horse. What should she do?

She and Helen were having wonderful experiences,

meeting famous people. They had been invited to the homes of Dr. Oliver Wendell Holmes and of John Greenleaf Whittier. These great men had seemed to think Annie every bit as wonderful as Helen, and this had warmed Annie's heart. Was she just being selfish, wanting to stay?

When she was in the midst of this Boston-Tuscumbia debate with herself, something new came up which decided the issue for her.

Helen heard about a little blind and deaf girl in Norway who had learned to speak. A woman named Mrs. Lamson, who came to speak to the children at Perkins, told them the story of Ragnhild Kaata.

"If she could do it, I can! I can do anything anybody else can!" Helen spelled into Annie's hand in an ecstasy of excitement.

Annie, herself, felt something of the same excitement. "I will talk to the lady. We will see," Annie spelled back.

"Now! Now!" Helen demanded imperiously.

"When she has finished talking to the students we will invite her in to have tea with us."

Mrs. Hopkins joined them for tea. Yes, there was a Miss Sarah Fuller in Boston who taught lipreading and articulation. Mrs. Lamson suggested that Annie and Helen go to see her.

Annie could hardly get Helen to sleep that night, so great was the girl's agitation. Nothing would do but that they should see Miss Fuller the very next day.

Before they returned to Perkins, Helen had had her first lesson in speech.

Annie observed Miss Fuller carefully at each lesson, and soon she felt that she knew the technique well enough to proceed with the lessons herself. The money which came from Captain Keller was scarcely adequate for the continuation of private lessons.

"Do you realize what you're letting yourself in for?" asked Mrs. Hopkins when they had returned from their eleventh lesson and Annie said it had been their last.

"Well, at least I don't have to strain me eyes at this," Annie laughed.

"No, but I'll venture you'll strain every nerve in your body."

Often in the weeks that followed, Annie thought of Mrs. Hopkins' prediction. Surely this was the hardest work she had ever done! The strange, guttural sounds which issued from Helen's throat tore at her heart.

At the end of six weeks of struggle Annie felt justified in writing Mr. Anagnos: "Helen can talk with her mouth." Not only could she now say words which were understandable, but she could utter whole sentences that Annie, at least, could understand, as could Mrs. Hopkins and some of the more interested teachers at Perkins.

Annie's nerves were frayed with the effort. When a reporter from the *Boston Journal* came to interview her he inadvertently aroused her Irish temper when he referred to Helen as "a regular pupil of Perkins Institute."

"She is *not* a regular pupil of Perkins Institute!" she flared. "She is *my* pupil. I have the sole charge of her, and my salary is paid by her father."

Little did she realize what a hornet's nest she was stirring up. The reporter used her words to enhance his story, and the next day she was called before the Perkins Board of Trustees.

"Oh, wouldn't ye know I'd open me big mouth and put me foot in it?" she stormed to Mrs. Hopkins.

She was soon to learn that she had done more than this. The Board of Trustees was stern. The Board of Trustees was stony. "It seems as if you are biting the hand that fed you, Miss Sullivan."

"But I didn't mean it that way. She *is* my charge."

When the meeting was over the Trustees were as stony as ever, and Annie was even more upset.

"Why, they aren't even going to let us be on the commencement program!" she cried to her friend.

"I wouldn't worry about that."

"But they think me ungrateful." Annie was in despair. She sat up far into the night composing a letter of apology. The next morning she copied and posted it. "I think Helen and I will pack," she said unhappily to Mrs. Hopkins. "We certainly don't want to be around here at commencement sitting in the audience when we'd been announced as a part of the program."

Helen was delighted at the thought of returning home

to "see" her loved ones, especially a new baby brother.

They had kept the knowledge of her learning to talk a secret which was to be sprung on the family upon their return. Annie was in a state of dejection during the whole tedious journey south.

She forgot her own disgruntlement, however, when she saw tears of joy running down Mrs. Keller's cheeks at the word "Mama" from Helen's lips.

XIX. Without Benefit of Pay

The summer, Annie's third at Tuscumbia, did not prove to be her best, despite the Kellers' joy at Helen's learning to speak. It was not that the Kellers were not appreciative of what Annie had done; even Captain Keller seemed to have capitulated. It was rather that she herself was unhappy about Helen, torn with anxiety and self-accusation. For the first time since Annie had known her, Helen was not well. Annie had dispensed with regular lessons again but she could not slow Helen's questioning and her feverish desire to learn. Added to this were the demands of her constant effort to speak.

"I don't know what we're going to do with her," Annie said to Mrs. Keller one hot day. "She gets more nervous every day."

"We've been talking of going to the mountains," Mrs. Keller replied. "It would be cooler, and perhaps we would all feel better."

The mountain cabin to which they went was a delight. Annie and Helen took long walks in the woods, but Helen's health did not improve.

"Do you think I've pushed her too fast?" Annie asked Mrs. Keller, her face troubled.

"My dear," Mrs. Keller said kindly, "you haven't pushed her at all. You've just kept up with her, and I don't know how you've managed to do that. Not one person in a thousand could."

Annie sighed. "I don't think I should ever have started the speech lessons, but she just *demanded* it."

"Don't blame yourself, Annie."

Annie did blame herself, however. Helen had been her sole responsibility, and something had gone wrong.

While they were still in the mountains a letter came from Mr. Anagnos. He was back in the United States and would like to have Annie and Helen come back for another year at Perkins.

"Well," Annie thought, "he said nothing about my trouble with the trustees. *He* must not feel that I was biting the hand that fed me."

It gave her a warm feeling to think he did not blame her and that he wanted them. Yes, she would like to spend another pleasant winter at Perkins with him there. She must think of Helen, however, and she was sure it would not be good for her to attempt school again. In fact, she frequently found herself wondering if the regular classroom routine of the preceding year might not have something to do with Helen's nervous state. She wrote Mr. Anagnos that she was sorry, but she did not think it wise for them to come.

When they returned to Tuscumbia in September, however, there was another letter waiting for her. "Why don't you come anyway," Mr. Anagnos had written, "even if you don't want to put Helen in school? She would have the pleasure of associating with the other children, and I would have the pleasure of associating with you. The concert season will soon be opening . . ." Annie smiled. She carried the letter about with her for several days, thinking about it. Finally, she broached the subject to the Kellers.

To her surprise, Captain Keller left the decision entirely to her. "Whatever you think best, Miss Annie," he said.

At last, she decided to go.

"Oh, Teacher, it's so much fun to be going back to see all the little blind children," Helen croaked in her strange, guttural voice when they were on the train.

People stared at them curiously. Annie heard someone say, "I do believe that's Helen Keller."

"Shh, dear. Let's just think with our fingers while we're on the train," Annie spelled into her hand. She hated the way Helen was becoming a public curiosity. She hated having to answer people's questions. She wanted Helen's life to be as nearly normal as possible, but it seemed to her that this was becoming more and more *im*possible.

She and Mr. Anagnos came very close to a quarrel over her attitude once that winter. He had insisted upon Annie's writing a report of Helen's progress for the annual Perkins Institute résumé of the preceding year.

When the publication appeared reporters came to interview him, and he called for Annie to bring Helen to his office. She did not know what he wanted until it was too late. When she saw the reporters she froze.

"I don't see why you want to be so reticent," Mr. Anagnos challenged her after the reporters had left.

"I don't see why you want to exploit the child," Annie retorted hotly.

When the interview was published she was furious. She went to Mr. Anagnos, news sheet in hand. "I'm going to take her back to Tuscumbia," she announced.

"Now don't be hasty," Mr. Anagnos protested.

"It isn't even true," she stormed. "It says she talks fluently. You know yourself that it is difficult to understand her. The reporters wouldn't have known what she was trying to say at all if we hadn't interpreted for them. Besides—and this is what really gets my Irish up —they make her sound like a combination of a genius and some oddity that belongs in a circus."

"Now, Annie, don't get upset. You're just touchy on the subject. It's only right that the public should know what amazing progress Helen has made. We need all the money we can get, you know, to help in our work with the blind."

Annie gave him a withering look and left.

In other ways this year was not as happy as the others at Perkins had been. Besides the problem of fighting publicity, Annie was still uncertain about the wisdom of having Helen in school. She had not let her start any classes until late November, and even then she was beset by doubts.

One night she talked it over with Mrs. Hopkins. "The thing that worries me is the responsibility," she said, pacing the floor. "I used to chafe at the bit when Captain Keller wouldn't let me do what I wanted to do with Helen, and now that he seems to have turned her over to me completely, making the decisions frightens me."

"It is a big responsibility," Mrs. Hopkins admitted. "But it seems to me you are doing very well."

Annie shook her head. "Molding a life—that's what it amounts to. And I'm not sure that any human being has a right to do that."

Mrs. Hopkins smiled. "It seems to me that Helen has a very strong mind and will of her own. I don't believe I'd worry about that."

"It's true. She does. But did you ever stop to think that really *I* am the one—you might almost say I am the *only* one who fashions the ideas that go into her mind? Even in the classes she attends here at Perkins, *I* interpret to her. I . . . I . . . I—and I'm *not God!*" she ended explosively.

She was glad to see the school year end. "I just don't know about schools," she mumbled as she was packing for their return to Tuscumbia.

"What don't you know about schools?" Mrs. Hopkins asked.

"I just don't know about schools and Helen."

She had other worries waiting for her when she reached Tuscumbia, worries that she had not in any sense anticipated while in Boston.

She felt that something was wrong even as they were met at the train, but she couldn't put her finger on what it was. "Just me Irish intuition workin' overtime, I guess," she told herself when they were back at the Kellers' house. Certainly Helen was happy, and she kept Annie busy that first day. They must visit every old friend on the place—every little Negro playmate, every single animal, all their favorite haunts. By the end of the day Annie was so tired that she decided she couldn't even write to Mr. Anagnos and Mrs. Hopkins to report their safe arrival. "I'm going right to bed," she told Helen when they came in from their final round after supper.

Helen laughed and ran up the stairs ahead of her.

"She does seem much better physically," Annie said to herself. "I thought her mother would remark about it, but she hasn't said a word."

Again that strange premonition of something wrong touched her. Mrs. Keller had not seemed herself.

Annie did not have long to wait or wonder. She had no more than reached her room when Mildred knocked on her door. "Baby Mildred," Annie thought, smiling, as she opened the door to her. The child was going on five now, as Helen was going on twelve, no longer a baby, but Annie adored her.

"Daddy wants you to come to his office, please," she said to Annie, then danced into the room to play with Helen, whom she was overjoyed to have home.

Annie looked at the two of them together, happiness in her heart. The day after she had first arrived at Tuscumbia Helen had deliberately tipped over Mildred's cradle, dumping the baby out on her head. Mrs. Keller had explained to Annie that someone had to watch the baby continuously as Helen was very jealous. The contrast between their relationship then and now was great.

"Sit down, Miss Annie," Captain Keller said when Annie reached his study. "I have something to say to you which is very difficult to say."

"He has aged this past year," Annie thought. What did he have to say to her that would be difficult? He wasn't about to fire her again, was he?

"When you first came to us," he began, "we settled on a monthly salary for you. It was little enough, but it was all that I could pay. Now I am faced with the sad duty of having to tell you I can't pay—even that."

Annie waited, her heart racing. What was he trying to tell her?

"This past winter, while you were away," he went on slowly, "I lost the newspaper. And, of course, with the change in the White House, I no longer have my other position. All I have left is this place, and it barely feeds my rather large family and the servants and hands."

Annie sat stunned. She swallowed but she could not speak.

"I simply can't keep you on, Miss Annie. It is a tragedy for Helen, but you have given her so much . . ."

Finally Annie found her voice. "You mean ye—ye couldn't even feed me?" she stammered.

Captain Keller smiled for the first time. "There'll always be food on our table for you, Annie Sullivan," he said. "But I can't pay your salary, small as it is."

"If ye'll feed me," she replied, "I'll stay."

XX. *Accusations*

Annie had been fearful that Captain Keller's financial difficulties would mean the family must spend the summer in the heat at Tuscumbia. So she was much pleased one breathless morning when the Captain said at breakfast, "I think it's about time you women folk remove to Fern Quarry. This heat is becoming unbearable." The surprise which Annie felt must have shown in her face for Captain Keller said, "Fern Quarry belongs to my family, Miss Annie, and we at Tuscumbia seem to be the only ones who care to use it."

"Fine!" Annie cried. "I'm glad to get included in the Tuscumbia branch. I love it at Fern Quarry."

"I wish we could all go," Mrs. Keller said, wistfully. "I hate having you and the boys stay here in the heat."

"We have our work to do," The Captain said firmly.

James pushed his chair back from the table. "Heat or no heat, we have our work to do. And if you will excuse me, I will be about mine."

Annie smiled at him. "See that you do it!" she said. She could joke with him now. He was no longer the sullen, sarcastic youth who had met her at the train four years before. He had taken a job in town this summer, and Simpson had assumed supervision of the field hands. Simpson was seventeen now. Annie looked at him approvingly. He was a fine lad, well built, quiet, and dependable. She liked this household of which she was a member; she knew that its members liked and respected her. But this had not come about all at once. "Well, it's a good thing I'm happy with *them*," she thought. "They're all the life I have." She had never been accepted in Tuscumbia outside the Keller family, and now her life in Boston would be cut off because of lack of funds.

"May I tell Helen we're going to Fern Quarry soon?" she asked.

"Of course," the Captain replied.

She spelled the good news into Helen's hand and was rewarded by Helen's joyous response. She jumped up and down in her chair, clapping her hands.

"You do love the mountains!" Annie remarked.

The feminine half of the Keller household stayed longer than usual in the mountain cabin that summer.

One weekend in September, when Captain Keller and the boys had come for a brief respite, Mrs. Keller said, "Well, I suppose we should be thinking about coming home."

Captain Keller looked around at them all and smiled. "I've never seen you looking better, my dear," he said to his wife. "And Helen is radiant. Miss Annie and Mildred look the picture of health. Why come down yet awhile? It is still very hot. Up here, with Viney to look after you and the mountain air to brace you, there is no question but that you're all better off than at Tuscumbia. Stay as long as you like."

So they stayed on and the air grew crisp and the leaves began to turn. Annie felt a resurgence of energy. As she and Helen walked through the woods and Annie described the red and the gold of the autumn foliage to her pupil, she thought, "Helen's become the picture of health again." She was no longer nervous. She slept long hours and awoke pulsating with anticipation of each new day. Annie had done little with lessons since they had come to Fern Quarry, but now she must think about them again. There was no money with which to return to Perkins. "I'm going to need more advanced books this year," she thought.

She would write Mr. Anagnos. Perhaps he could help her with the problem of books. There might be old ones or extra ones at Perkins that she could borrow.

It was the middle of October before they returned to Tuscumbia. Annie found a letter waiting for her from Mr. Anagnos. Of course he would see that she got the books she needed, but certainly he could not think of her and Helen's remaining in Tuscumbia all winter. "Pray do not have the least anxiety about the future," he wrote. "Be Captain Keller's circumstances what they may, Helen and you will not be allowed to suffer." He would send the money for their trip any time that Annie would say the word. Perkins was not the same without them there. Boston was not the same without Annie Sullivan.

Annie thought about the letter for a long time, but she did not mention it to the Kellers. She was afraid of hurting Captain Keller's pride—and she did not like the idea of being "beholden" to Mr. Anagnos, herself. Yet, as always, there was Helen to be considered. Again Annie began warring within herself. Should she forget Captain Keller and herself? Certainly Helen was fast getting beyond the point where Annie Sullivan could handle her education singlehandedly. So what was she to do? Still she delayed.

One November morning Annie noticed that Helen was very intent on something she was writing on her Braille slate. She had set her no task to do and, curious, went to see what she was about. Feeling Annie's presence, Helen stopped long enough to spell into her hand, "I'm writing a story for Mr. Anagnos. It's for his birthday."

Annie went away, smiling to herself. To think Helen had remembered Mr. Anagnos' birthday! She would be interested to see the story. She thought Helen wrote very well for a child. Part of the credit she could take herself, for she had been a hard taskmistress, making Helen write things over and over until they were perfect. For Helen's imagination and ability to visualize, however, she could certainly take no credit.

Even though she had come to expect good writing from Helen, she felt a growing wonder as she read this

174

story after Helen had completed it. For a child not yet twelve . . . "This is *very* good, Helen," she said.

"Oh, do you like it?" Helen was ecstatic. Annie had noted the warm glow in her cheeks as she worked; now she, too, felt something of this glow, reflected. Certainly it was the glow of satisfaction born of creating something and knowing it was good. Vicariously, Annie too was knowing this satisfaction. "Your father would like to hear this. Let's read it to the family at dinner tonight."

"Oh, let's!"

Before they took it in to read to the others Annie suggested just one change. Helen had called it "Autumn Leaves." "Since the main character in your story is The Frost King, I'd like to see you use that for your title." Helen nodded assent.

Annie had felt certain that the little story would bring pleasure to Captain Keller, with his background as a journalist, and she was right. He praised Helen extravagantly. "I do believe I'm going to have a writer in the family," he said.

"You didn't read that some place, did you?" asked James.

"Of course not!" Helen replied.

"It really is good, isn't it?" Mrs. Keller said, awed.

"I thought so. Very!" Annie said proudly.

Helen copied the little story in her square script and with her own hand put it into the mailbox, addressed to Mr. Anagnos.

"She's very pleased with herself," Annie said to Mrs. Keller. "I don't know when I've ever seen a mood last so long with her. It would be wonderful, wouldn't it," she mused, "if she *should* become a writer?"

Mrs. Keller smiled. She was content, just seeing Helen develop into a normal, happy girl.

Mr. Anagnos was as pleased as the others. "It's wonderful," he wrote. "I am going to include it in the Annual Report I'm working on. It is further evidence of the genius Helen has been exhibiting all along." Then he repeated his request that Annie and Helen come to Perkins "for a visit." Dr. Bell was going to be in Boston; he would like to see them, too. This time Mr. Anagnos included railroad tickets. Annie could no longer keep still about the matter. Somewhat to her surprise, Captain Keller seemed pleased rather than offended when she mentioned it. Helen, as usual when a trip was in the offing, was extravagantly happy. Once the decision had been made, Annie, too, was happy about it.

She did not anticipate the trouble that lay ahead, however, or there would have been no joy in her heart.

They arrived at Perkins in early February. The Perkins Institute children were planning a patriotic pageant for Washington's Birthday, and Helen was given a part. She became immediately a regular member of the Perkins family again—immediately, but only briefly.

While Helen was practicing her part and being measured for her costume, Mr. Anagnos was making

Annie happy to be "at home" again. It seemed to her that every day he planned some little pleasantry to make her day bright. She was not surprised when he said one day, "Won't you come into my office? I have something for you." Annie noted the pleased expression on his face. She followed him in, and he handed her an open magazine. She glanced at the page and read, " 'The Frost King,' by Helen Keller."

"Oh, you sent it to a magazine!" she exclaimed.

"And they published it—*The Mentor!* Didn't I tell you the story was good enough to have been written by an adult author with all of his five senses?"

Annie nodded. "This *is* nice; it will please Helen." She couldn't help being appreciative of all Mr. Anagnos was doing for her and Helen. "Thank you," she added and impulsively took his hand.

He seized both her hands in his and pressed them. "Annie . . ."

There was a tap at the door. He dropped her hands, and Annie left the room.

"You may take the magazine with you," he called.

Annie had been watching the excitement build in Helen again. And in her own mind the old battle was beginning. "Schools!" she thought in disgust. "I just don't think they're for Helen. And yet, what am I to do?" She was in this confused state when, a few days later, Mr. Anagnos sent for her again.

She was glad. A chat in his office would divert her mind

from her troubles, and perhaps he had some happy plan for the evening.

The moment she entered his office, her anticipation vanished. He was holding out a magazine, and his face was as stony as those of the trustees had been when she had inadvertently displeased them.

What had she done?

She found herself feeling guilty, as she used to feel when she was a pupil at Perkins and had been sent to the headmaster's office to be disciplined. In another minute, however, she felt as rebellious as she had used to feel.

Without saying a word, she read the article he handed her. It was a review of "The Frost King"—a review and an accusation! As she read, Annie could feel the blood draining from her face.

Finally she realized that Mr. Anagnos was speaking. His voice and his eyes were icy. "Probably the child did not realize that it was wrong. A child so pure and lovely as Helen, who doesn't even know Evil exists . . . She wouldn't know what plagiarism is. But *you,* Annie Sullivan! To think you would perpetrate such a fraud . . . And on *me!*"

Annie stared at him in disbelief. Then in a tone of suppressed fury, her eyes blazing in her white face, she hissed, *"How dare you? How dare you!"* She threw the magazine on his desk and whirled from the room.

XXI. Dr. Bell

Dr. Bell arrived at Perkins. It always made Annie feel better to be in his presence, for he made her lose her sense of inferiority. With him she could be herself.

She had been ready to pack and take Helen home immediately the night after Mr. Anagnos had accused her of knowing that Helen's story was not original. The words of the article he had handed her were seared on her brain: "Many passages in this story are identical with passages of 'Frost Fairies,' a story written by Miss Margaret T. Canby and published in 1873 in a volume entitled *Birdie and His Fairy Friends*. The parallel passages are quoted here."

How had it happened?

Annie blamed herself, for surely every story that had been read to Helen she had read and every book that had been put in Helen's hands she had placed there. Yet she had no recollection of ever having read or seen such a story as this. How was it possible that the plot and even the very phrasing of Helen's story corresponded to that of Miss Canby's?

Mrs. Hopkins had counseled her to remain at Perkins and see the whole thing through. "It will look as if you have something to run away from if you leave," she said.

Telling Helen what had happened was the hardest thing Annie Sullivan had ever had to do. She watched the child's face blanch when she understood what her teacher was trying to tell her. Annie's own heart twisted with pain.

"But it's *my* story! It's mine!" Helen kept crying over and over.

Annie knelt and took Helen in her arms. But she could not reach her. Suddenly the child began to sob. Annie laid her on the bed and held her close. After a time Helen's hand reached for Annie's. "Don't they know that I love the beautiful truth?" her fingers fluttered.

Annie could have killed "them."

"Teacher knows it, darling," she spelled back. "And I will try to make them understand."

Annie was able to make no one understand anything. "They don't want to understand!" she cried to Mrs. Hopkins. She felt as if she and Helen were in the enemy camp with no means of escape.

Then Dr. Bell came.

"Oh, I'm so glad to see you!" Annie said as he held both her hands tightly in his.

He looked at her searchingly. "Don't tell me Annie Sullivan has lost her spirit," he said.

"Sure an' it's enough to take the heart out of anyone," she replied, "the way they're browbeating that poor, innocent child. Why, do you know what they did yesterday? They put Helen through a two-hour inquisition! That's what they did! And they wouldn't even let me in the room! Mrs. Hopkins said we should stay, but I wish I'd taken her out of here the minute Mr. Anagnos showed me that article. It's inhuman, that's what it is!"

Annie stopped for breath.

Dr. Bell shook his head. "It's most regrettable. Most regrettable," he said.

"Won't ye sit down?" Annie said. "I'm sorry. I'm even forgettin' me manners."

Dr. Bell smiled and seated himself. "Now, let's look at this thing rationally," he advised. "You know that Helen has an amazing memory. You know that she has learned language by groups of words, sentences, rather than by single, isolated words. And this is right. In this you made a discovery for which the world can never thank you enough. It is already beginning to be felt in the teaching of the deaf."

"But what have I done to me precious Helen?" Annie moaned.

"You've opened the world to her, of course. You know that. Just don't lose sight of it in the heat of the moment. Now let's see what's to be done."

Annie was silent.

"Obviously, the child had either read the story some place—which would mean that it's in Braille—or someone had read it to her. It had lain dormant in her brain until you started telling her about the beauty of the autumn foliage in the mountains last fall. Then it came back to her, and she had—and has—no recollection of its having been put *into* her mind. So she can't realize that it's not her own creation."

"She can't even *believe* it," Annie put in.

Dr. Bell nodded. "We must instigate a careful search," he said, "to find the book, to find when and under what circumstances the story was first introduced to her. Then we must explain to the press what has happened and hope people will understand."

Annie's lip curled bitterly. "People at Perkins won't. They don't want to."

"Did it ever occur to you that there is such a thing as jealousy in the world?"

Annie stared at him.

"Now," he went on in a matter-of-fact tone, "we shall start our search. I would suggest that, first, all the books in the Perkins library be checked. At the same time, the books in the Keller library at Tuscumbia."

It was Mrs. Hopkins who finally came up with the answer. Her library had been searched along with the others, as Helen had spent considerable time at the Cape on summer visits, but it disclosed no trace of "The Frost Fairies."

"You know, though," Mrs. Hopkins mused, "I've given a number of Florence's children's books away. I wonder . . ."

She contacted friends to whom she had given her daughter's books. At last "The Frost Fairies" came to light. Margaret Canby's *Birdie and His Fairy Friends* was among the books.

"I have absolutely no recollection of reading the story to her," Mrs. Hopkins said, "but I must have—that time you were having your eyes treated. I know I did read to her to try to keep her amused. But that story—I don't remember it at all."

Annie sighed in relief.

"Well, at least they can't blame you any longer!" Mrs. Hopkins said.

Annie, though, could not see that the atmosphere at Perkins changed perceptibly after their discovery. And she could never, never forgive Mr. Anagnos. Her one desire was to get away from Perkins, "now that we've sweated it out," she said to Mrs. Hopkins.

Again, it was her friend Dr. Alexander Graham Bell who opened the way.

"I have a job for you," he told her.

"As if I didn't have job enough," Annie protested, "especially now. You've no idea how deeply this has hurt Helen."

"I think I have. And Annie Sullivan. But both these people are of the ilk to come out of difficulties the stronger for the experience. Now, about this job . . ."

Annie sighed, folded her hands, and sat down to listen.

". . . or perhaps you will think it is two jobs," Dr. Bell said, smiling. "The *Youth's Companion* wants Helen to write a little story of her life for their publication."

Annie cringed.

"I know it will not be easy. But somehow it must be done. She must get over her fear. And you must get over yours. This must not be the end of Helen's writing. You know as well as I that when you've been thrown from a horse, you must climb on his back again immediately and . . ."

"If you can," Annie said.

"Helen can," Dr. Bell replied firmly. "You must see to it that she does."

Annie sighed shakily.

"And that is not all," Dr. Bell added. "It is high time that the world has an accurate account of the methods you have used in teaching Helen because . . ."

Annie started to protest.

He put out his hand to stop her. "No, not to be garbled and made into eulogies in Perkins reports, nor to be twisted by the press, but an actual, careful account of what you have done. Next year at the meeting of the Association to Promote the Teaching of Speech to the Deaf, I want you to read your own account. I want you to start working on it immediately. I think you and Helen might like a little fresh country air while you work on your projects, so I'm sending you back to Tuscumbia."

He held out two train tickets.

Annie could not speak for the lump in her throat.

The double task Dr. Bell had assigned to her was one

of the most difficult she would ever have to face. Yet she knew that he was right.

It took some months, but by the time Dr. Bell sent for Annie to come to Chautauqua, New York, to read the paper, it had been carefully prepared, and Helen's brief account of her life had been sent off to the *Youth's Companion*. "You are to bring Helen with you," Dr. Bell wrote. "Tell Captain Keller that we have something in mind for her further education. I shall tell you about it when I see you."

Annie was dressed and ready to go to the meeting. Her paper was in her hands—but her hands were trembling. When Dr. Bell came to the door to pick her up she looked at him pleadingly. "Would you mind *very* much reading my paper for me?" she asked, holding it toward him.

Seeing how pale she was and how the paper trembled in her hands, he shook his head indulgently and took it from her. "Annie Sullivan," he said, "I wish I could give you a small fraction of the confidence *I* have in you so that you might have a little in yourself."

XXII. Fears

Annie was literally surrounded by an excited group of dedicated men and women whose chief interest was the teaching of speech to the deaf. At the moment, however, their chief interest was Annie Sullivan.

Dr. Bell had read Annie's speech for her, but he had insisted that she sit on the platform with him. In addition, he gave her full credit not only for the paper but for the method of teaching which it revealed. Now the audience, which had listened with growing excitement, crowded about Annie, asking eager questions, shaking her hand in congratulation, expressing their admiration and appreciation. Annie was no longer pale. She was flushed with embarrassment. "It isn't anything wonderful," she kept repeating. "I just observed how normal children learned language, and then I adapted it to Helen's especial needs."

She saw that Dr. Bell was standing by, a pleased smile on his face, with two men he was waiting to introduce to her. She excused herself from the others and stepped to his side. "Dr. Humason. Mr. Wright," he said, "Miss Annie Sullivan, whom I am proud to call my friend."

"He's as Irish as the Irish," she said to the two, shaking

her head. "Anybody'd know 'tis the other way 'round. I'm the proud one, to be able to call the great Dr. Alexander Graham Bell a friend." Her voice was humble, and the respect, admiration, and gratitude which mingled in her feelings for Dr. Bell rang out clearly.

The men smiled at her.

"Dr. Humason and Mr. Wright are opening a school in New York City, Annie," Dr. Bell explained, "with the explicit purpose of teaching oral language to the deaf. We thought you might be interested in taking Helen there for some work. Her speaking voice could perhaps be improved, and, as you have done some work along this line yourself, you could undoubtedly be of help to these gentlemen in their undertaking."

Annie drew a long breath. So Dr. Bell had had a double motive in asking her to come to New York!

This would take a little consideration, but at the moment it sounded like a good idea. She had reached the point where she didn't know what to do about Helen's education, and here was a hand reaching out to help her.

As she deliberated the matter that night and came to the decision to accept the offer, she smiled a bit ruefully. "The hand reaching out to help me seems more and more often to be the hand of Dr. Alexander Graham Bell," she thought. Then she said aloud, "Bless him."

She had reason to bless him many times in the months which followed. Though Annie saw to her sorrow that Helen's voice was not going to become normal, Helen was learning to speak more distinctly and was keeping up in her studies with students who were only deaf—not blind as well. Annie did not enjoy the restrictions of school routine, but she was pleased with Helen's progress in her studies. And there were other compensations.

"Never did I think to meet such famous people," she said to Dr. Bell one night when he had taken her and Helen to the theater. Dr. Bell had just said, "Miss Terry is a friend of mine. I'm going to take you to her dressing room to meet her."

Annie explained to Helen that Ellen Terry was one of the greatest actresses of the day and that they were going to have the privilege of meeting her.

When they went backstage Annie was aghast to hear Miss Terry say, "Miss Sullivan, I consider it a privilege to meet you. It makes me ashamed of my own life when I think what a wonderful thing you are doing with yours."

"But . . . , but . . . ," Annie stammered.

"You see, Annie Sullivan, in what high esteem the most wonderful of people hold you," Dr. Bell said gently.

"But no one else knows my shortcomings as well as I do," Annie laughed.

Annie and Helen met many other famous people during their two years in New York—Mark Twain, John D. Rockefeller, Woodrow Wilson, Andrew Carnegie. Of all the greats and the near-greats Annie met, however, she felt most drawn to Mark Twain. He had become her champion, and Helen's, even before they met him, for he was on their side in the "Frost King" controversy. He had written them a letter which Annie would cherish always, pointing out that every writer did, in a sense, what Helen had done, and so did every inventor and every other person who worked in any creative field.

Even so, Annie had not been prepared for the great, protective warmth of him and for the sincere homage he paid to Annie Sullivan when he met her.

"You're one of the real geniuses of this age," he said to her, his big hand on her shoulder, "and don't you ever forget it."

Annie blossomed under such genuine appreciation from people whom she knew to be truly great in their own right. On the surface, at least, she became more sure of herself, more poised, but underneath there was still the silent storm. Her own beginnings, the almshouse, the nightmare of losing Jimmie, the aloneness, her utter lack of the simplest opportunities, the great gaps in her education—all these, in her own mind, set her apart and made her inadequate.

So now, when she and Helen were leaving New York, when she had reached another point of crisis in regard to Helen, the storm within her seethed as of old. Helen was growing into young womanhood. She wanted to go to college. The final decision rested with Annie.

"I'm afraid," she admitted to herself, lying awake in the night. "I'm afraid she can't do it. She's never been educated in the regular way. She's never been trained with the idea of being prepared to enter college. And what about me? I couldn't help her. Why, I probably couldn't even understand what she was studying. I'd have to be her eyes, and just look at *my* eyes! It's too much! It's just too much to expect!"

"I want to go to Harvard," Helen said.

Annie laughed. "You know only men can go to Harvard."

"Oh, well, you know what I mean—where they have women . . ."

"Radcliffe," Annie said with a sigh.

Helen was serious, and Annie knew it. "And who am I to deny her the chance?" she asked herself. "Oh, but how I hate to think about it. Entrance exams! They have to pass entrance exams before they're even admitted. And I don't even know on what subjects."

Again she turned to Dr. Bell. Not only were there entrance examinations, he explained, but one had to make an application. One had to be accepted.

"Even to take the examinations?" Annie demanded indignantly.

"It amounts to that," Dr. Bell admitted.

Finally Annie wrote the letter to Radcliffe.

When the reply came she was almost afraid to open it. When she had read it, however, her temper flared. She decided that Helen should be given her chance. She would show them! The letter was not at all encouraging.

The authorities did not feel that it would be wise for Helen Keller to think in terms of Radcliffe. The entrance requirements were strict. The scholastic reputation of the college was high. The competition within the college was keen. If Miss Keller wished to go to college why did she not choose a less rigorous one whose intellectual standards would not be as difficult to meet?

"Perhaps they think we can't meet their academic standards!" Annie flared. Immediately she began looking for a good preparatory school where Helen could start getting ready for entrance examinations. In the meantime, she had little doubt that the influence of their good friend Dr. Bell, and others, would win the opportunity for Helen to take the examinations if she could be adequately prepared for them.

Of this last Annie was not sure. And would not failure be worse for Helen than not making the attempt?

Others, too, were doubtful, she discovered as she started a search for a preparatory school where Helen might be enrolled. There also was the problem of expense. Helen was sixteen now. For several years well-to-do friends who had taken a deep interest in her and Annie had given them financial aid. Annie seldom worried about money. "As long as we have enough to eat today, why worry about tomorrow?" she laughed.

Now, however, as she investigated this preparatory school and that, the problem of money loomed large before her. Preparatory schools were private. They were expensive. If they agreed to take her they would expect Helen Keller to pay as they would expect anyone else to pay.

Then word came from Tuscumbia which brought Helen her first real grief. Captain Keller, after a short illness, had died. The rest of the family—Mrs. Keller, Helen's half brothers, James and Simpson, her sister Mildred, even her small brother Phillips, and Annie as well —were all brought to a sense of great loss.

"She loved her father very deeply," Annie wrote Mrs. Hopkins. "He was perhaps too indulgent with her, but his tenderness for her touched something very deep within her, and it seems impossible to comfort her. I must find a school for her soon. I believe that only some such new interest will rouse her from the despondency into which she has sunk."

Annie found the place for which she was looking. At least she found a place which would accept Helen as a pupil—the Cambridge School for Young Ladies. Influential friends had helped persuade Mr. Gilman, the head of the school, that having Helen as a pupil might give his school a certain prestige. Wealthy friends had helped further in persuading him to accept her by offering to pay him well.

"It would be quite a feather in our cap, eh, Miss Sullivan," he said, as Annie at last filled out the actual registration blanks, "if we could get Miss Keller through the Radcliffe entrance examinations, which are reputed to be the most difficult anywhere in the country. Quite a feather in our cap!"

Annie did not like the contemplative gleam in his eyes as he said it. There were other things she was to like even less before she was through with Mr. Arthur Gilman.

XXIII. *Betrayal*

There was an interlude before the school term began. Annie was restless. She dreaded the ordeal ahead more than she dared admit to Helen, and there was something else gnawing at her that would not be stilled—something from her past.

She and Helen were visiting Dr. Bell and his secretary Mr. Hitz. Annie had come to love Mr. Hitz dearly— Mr. Hitz of the flowing white beard and fatherly wisdom. "I'd call you Father Time," she said to him one day, "only you're timeless. I'll call you Mon Pere."

The eyes behind the spectacles twinkled at her. "You are making of me a French Irishman?"

Annie laughed heartily. "What a thing to do to a fine Swiss friend!"

Now her "fine Swiss friend" showed the true depth of his friendship.

The four of them—Annie and Helen, Dr. Bell and Mr. Hitz—were alone together. Somehow the conversation turned to ancestors, and suddenly Annie said something which she would have said to no others in the world. "Sometimes I wish I knew . . ." she began and stopped, biting her lip. She glanced quickly from one to another and then, seeing the sympathy and the understanding in their eyes, went on. "I wish I knew something about my people. I had a little sister, you know. And I don't know whether my father is alive or dead. For a long time I didn't care. But now—sometimes I do wish that I had ties; sometimes it doesn't seem to make any difference. Then it seems to me that the importance is in whether one has become useful to society, not in what came before, good or bad. But I fluctuate like a weather vane in a high wind. Maybe a body just naturally craves some link with his beginnings. Silly, isn't it?" She laughed, but her laugh was unsteady.

"Feeding Hills isn't so far from Cambridge. Before you and Helen start school, would you like to have me take you there?" Mr. Hitz offered.

After much pondering, Annie decided to accept. Her sense of adventure possibly had something to do with her decision, as well as her natural curiosity. Then, too, she thought that going back might quiet some of the unrest within her. "But we will go incognito," she announced, for there was doubt in the back of her mind. "Not any of this knocking on people's doors and saying, 'I'm Annie Sullivan. Do ye know to what bad end me rascal of a father came?' "

Mr. Hitz smiled at her. "However you wish it," he said.

Annie's heart pounded, and her impulses were a series of darting contradictions on the bright October day when she and Mr. Hitz made the trip. As they drove over the red hills, still familiar to her in color and contour, she was torn between the bitter, cringing memories they roused in her and the somehow satisfying feeling that this, the place of her birth, was an actuality and not just a dream. "It—It, at least, makes me feel as if I'm real," she murmured.

Only once did she ask to get out of the carriage.

"That was my Cousin Anastasia's house," she said in a muted voice as they came over a hill. "I stayed there a while."

"Do you want me to go in with you?" asked Mr. Hitz when they had drawn up to the hitching post.

Annie shook her head. Her knees felt weak as she approached the door. She hesitated, thinking, "I don't know why I'm doing this."

A little, very old woman answered her knock. A shudder passed through Annie's body; she was quite certain this was her cousin. What courage she had had to explore her origins instantly vanished. Even the conflict within her as to whether she should do so ceased. Instead, she was overwhelmed with the remembrances of the shabbiness, the abject humility of being unwanted, shunted, and of the indignities of her childhood. So she suddenly invented a story: "I—I—We are writing a book about the early settlers of this region. I wonder if you could tell us anything about . . ." She couldn't say "the Sullivans." She couldn't. ". . . about a family by the name of O'Leary."

The old lady had waited, peering intently up into her face.

"Not hereabouts," she answered, shaking her head so that the white curls, peeking from under her starched cap, bobbed. She did not take her eyes off Annie's face as Annie's eyes darted quickly about the room which formed a backdrop for the little figure in the doorway. There once had been a lovely, blue-eyed doll under a Christmas tree over there. And this was the door through which she and Jimmie had gone to Tewksbury—Tewksbury Almshouse—Tewksbury . . .

"Thank you. I'm sorry to have troubled you."

Annie fled.

"It was my Cousin Anastasia. I know it was," she said when she was back in the carriage. She pressed her hands hard over her eyes. "And I think she knew me."

"Did you ask . . . ?"

Silently Annie shook her head.

They went back to Cambridge and Mr. Gilman's School for Young Ladies. Annie never again spoke of going to Feeding Hills.

She was too busy after school started to spend much time thinking about anything but Helen's studies. As before, Annie attended every class with her, spelling constantly into her hand what the teachers and the other students said. In the evening she must read to her from the many required sources which were not attainable in Braille. It was as confining as she had anticipated and had it not been for Helen's pleasure in associating with other girls her own age, and the fact that she was making obvious headway with her lessons, Annie could not have borne it.

There was a joyous break at Christmastime when Mrs. Keller and Mildred came to visit them. Much to everyone's surprise, Mr. Gilman invited Mildred to remain as a guest student.

"It's quite out of character," Annie said to Mrs. Keller.

"I don't understand it," Mrs. Keller admitted.

"Nor I," said Annie. "He certainly didn't offer Helen and me any such consideration! If it hadn't been for our friend Mrs. Hutton and the committee she put to raising funds for Helen's education, I'm sure he wouldn't even have considered taking us. Full fees are being paid from the fund. This I know."

At any rate, Annie was happy to have Mildred remain. She herself adored the girl, as she did all the young Kellers. To see Helen's and Mildred's joy now at being together was enough to lift anyone's heart.

As the end of the school year approached and the time drew near for Helen to take her preliminary examinations, Annie's tension mounted to an almost unendurable pitch. She couldn't eat. She couldn't sleep. She was using her eyes constantly, helping Helen with her final cramming, and she was paying for it. The old headaches returned.

Students desiring admission to Radcliffe, like those

seeking admission to Harvard, had to pass examinations in sixteen hours of college preparatory courses, twelve of which were termed "elementary" and four "advanced."

"It's all 'advanced' as far as I can see," Annie sighed to Mildred.

They had decided that Helen would take the examinations in German, French, Latin, English, Greek, and Roman history, deferring those in her more difficult subjects to a later date. June 29, 1897, was the date of the first examination.

Annie died a thousand deaths when she was told she could not read the examinations to Helen. "No. This would be impossible. Under these circumstances, it could well be Annie Sullivan instead of Helen Keller who would be taking the examinations for entrance."

This lack of trust was bad enough, but it annoyed her even more when she learned that Mr. Gilman would be allowed to read the examinations to Helen, who would do the answers on her typewriter. The two of them, Helen and Mr. Gilman, would be in a room alone. "Well, so *he's* to be trusted and I am not!" Annie laughed ironically.

The examinations were taken over a period of five days, and by the end of the fifth day Annie was in a state of near collapse.

Surely Annie's joy and satisfaction were as great as her pupil's when word came that Helen had passed all the examinations "with honors."

Mr. Gilman had originally contended that Helen should take five years for her preparation for college. Annie and the assistant principal of the school had argued for three. They had compromised at four. Now Annie again had hopes of making it in three.

When the girls came back to begin the second year, they came with confidence and enthusiasm bred of Helen's success in the examinations so far. This year it would be necessary for her to concentrate on mathematics, an area which had always been difficult for her. Still they were happy. Mildred was with them again, and the three were gay, though far from carefree.

Geometry caused Helen the most trouble. Annie devised a set of wires which she would form into triangles or other figures with which they were working.

One evening in exasperation, Helen scattered the wire figures Annie had carefully framed for her. Annie and Mildred looked at each other.

"You're tired," Annie said. "Tomorrow is Friday. Let's just forget school tomorrow, and you stay in bed and catch up on your sleep."

It seemed to Annie a very sensible thing to do, but it opened a breach that Mr. Gilman had apparently just been waiting for. He called Annie into his office. "You are working Helen far too hard," he said. "You are ruining her health. I insist that she drop two of her subjects."

Annie argued, but at last she gave in. "He's just trying

to make sure she'll be in his school four years," she said hotly to herself. She had again broached the possibility of Helen's finishing in three years when they had registered that fall. "He's getting a nice lot of publicity out of having her here, and it's paying big dividends. That's why he's willing to have Mildred, too," she thought.

Annie was never one to disguise her feelings, and the disagreement between her and Mr. Gilman grew as the semester went on. From Mrs. Keller herself Annie learned that the headmaster had written Helen's mother that she was pushing Helen brutally, that she was ruining her health.

On December 9, when the girls were beginning to look forward to the Christmas holidays, the blow fell. Mr. Gilman summoned Annie to his office. Not knowing what was coming, she, nevertheless, felt sure that it would be seriously unpleasant. "Why must it always be like this?" she thought. "Why am I forever being dumped into a boiling pot?"

Mr. Gilman spoke, "Miss Sullivan, your services are no longer needed here. From now on, I shall take over the guidance of Helen's education."

Annie's mouth dropped open. "What are you talking about?" she finally managed to ask.

"I do not want you here any longer."

Annie's eyes blazed. "Then I shall take Helen and Mildred and leave at once."

"You will do no such thing."

"What?!" Annie cried.

"*You* are to go. You will leave Helen and Mildred here."

He extended a telegram which Annie now realized he had been holding in his hand all along.

In stunned disbelief, Annie read:

Mr. Arthur Gilman
Cambridge School for Young Ladies

This is my authorization for you to take complete charge of my daughter, Helen Keller.

The message was signed "Kate Keller."

XXIV. Alone

It was impossible. It simply could not be true. It was a bad dream from which she would shortly awaken.

She made her way back to the rooms she shared with the Keller girls. She moved like a sleepwalker. When they demanded to know what the trouble was she tried to tell them. She found herself with two wildly hysterical girls on her hands.

"We won't let you go!"

"We'll go with you!"

Annie could not think. She was stunned. What to do? Very shortly Mr. Gilman himself appeared at the door.

"You will go immediately, Miss Sullivan," he said. "You can send for your possessions later."

There was no longer any question of what to do. Somehow she got into her hat and coat. Mr. Gilman extricated her from the clinging arms of Helen and Mildred, and she found herself outside, the door closed in her face.

Trembling from head to foot and physically sick with uncertainty and despair, she started to walk, having no idea where she was going or what she would do. Night and day for ten years she had been with Helen. Out of night she had brought her day. Mrs. Keller could not

mean this. There must be some mistake. How could her precious Helen get along without her? Did Mr. Gilman think *he* could do what she had done toward Helen's education? Attend every class with her? Spell every lecture into her hand? Read her countless books which were not obtainable in Braille? Was the man insane? Or was she? What had happened? As always when something went wrong, she tormented herself with the question: Was it her fault? If she hadn't argued and disagreed with Mr. Gilman, could this have been avoided? Yet she had given in on letting Helen drop the two subjects, much as she had disapproved.

Her mind was in an utter turmoil. She stumbled and found herself on her knees. She got up and went on, not feeling the cement burns on the palms of her hands where she had caught herself as she fell. There was a bitter wind, but she did not know it. It was growing dusk. The yellow flames of the gaslights were blossoming as the lamplighters reached up with their long poles. Annie did not see.

Suddenly something did reach her consciousness. She was walking beside the Charles River. As she saw it, her feet, almost without volition, started toward the bank. This was the answer. There was no other. She had come to the end.

She reached the brink of the river. She saw the lights reflected in the black water, making snaky chains. In her befuddled brain she saw them as chains which would encircle her neck and pull her down to oblivion. That was all she wanted—oblivion—yes.

Instinctively she lifted her arms to plunge in.

Then a physical force seemed to push her backwards. As clear as day, she heard a voice say, "No! you must go on! You must go on!"

Her arms dropped to her side. She felt utterly spent— as if she had been in that black water, struggling for hours to reach shore. She dropped down on a bench and held her whirling head in her hands.

"Go on! Go on! Go on!"

The words kept repeating themselves in her brain, hitting over and over like a hammer pounding a nail home.

"How can I?" she said aloud. "How can I go on?",

A policeman was going by on his beat. He stopped and stared at her.

"Are ye after bein' all right, lady?"

His Irish brogue somehow got through to her. She shook her head as if to clear it, rubbed her forehead hard with her finger tips, then looked up at him.

"I—I think I am," she said clearly.

She stood up. She felt very shaky, but she could think. She was not alone in Cambridge. She had friends there. She looked about her. She knew where she was. It was only a few blocks to the home of the Fullers', where she and Helen had often been entertained. She would go there. They would help her.

Mr. Fuller himself answered her knock.

"Miss Sullivan!" he cried. "What's happened?" He pulled her inside. Mrs. Fuller came running.

"Oh, my dear! Whatever is it?"

Annie's hair was streaming out from under her hat. She had thrust the hat on her head without looking when Mr. Gilman had told her to get out immediately. Her coat was open. Her bare hands were red with the cold. Her shoes were covered with mud. Her face was a white mask of anguish.

"You are frozen! Come in by the fire."

They half carried her to a rocking chair in the cozy living room, and Mrs. Fuller knelt to remove her wet shoes. "Get that footstool," she said to her husband. He placed it near the baseburner and pulled Annie's chair closer to the heat. Mrs. Fuller began rubbing her stiff hands.

"What is it? Can you tell us? Put the kettle on, Dick, so I can make her some hot tea."

Suddenly, in the midst of their kindness, Annie began to cry.

"It's Helen," she gasped. "Mr. Gilman . . . He . . . He's taken her away from me. He sent me off . . . He . . ."

"What!"

Mr. Fuller had returned from the kitchen, and his anger exploded in the single word.

Brokenly, with the Fullers interrupting with questions and expostulations, she told them what had happened.

As Mrs. Fuller soothed and mothered her, little by

little, Annie regained control of herself. But she kept coming back to the telegram. "Kate Keller . . . She's been my *friend*. I . . . I know she's appreciated more than anyone else in the world what I've done for Helen. I just can't believe she would turn against me!"

"She hasn't. I'm sure of it," Mrs. Fuller said stoutly.

Mr. Fuller had been pacing back and forth the length of the living room, his hands clasped tightly behind him. Now he stopped in front of the two women. "We must get busy at once," he said. "The first thing to do is to wire Mrs. Keller what has happened. Whatever the reason for her telegram I am sure she did not expect this."

He went for writing materials.

"And Dr. Bell," Annie said. "He's always been my mainstay. I guess I never could have gone on all these years if it hadn't been for him."

So they composed the telegrams.

"And the lady who's the chairman of the committee for Helen's education—shouldn't she be informed?" Mr. Fuller asked.

"Yes, I think so. Mrs. Hutton. Oh, you're so kind! I couldn't think at all what to do."

"No wonder," observed Mrs. Fuller. "Oh, that man! I never heard of such an inhumane thing!"

"And Mr. Joseph Chamberlin. He's close. He's in Boston."

"Oh, the Mr. Chamberlin of the *Boston Transcript?*"

"Sure and the same. He's been our very good friend

for years. And his wife. And their children. We've spent weeks at a time with them at their farm at Wrentham."

Mr. Fuller sent off the wires, and Mrs. Fuller got Annie to bed.

When Annie awoke, the sun was already streaming in the window. For a minute she couldn't think where she was nor what was causing the sense of heaviness which seemed to be pressing in on her from all sides. Then she remembered. She jumped out of bed and into her clothes, noting that her shoes had been cleaned and her stockings washed.

"Oh, bless them!" she said aloud.

This morning she knew exactly what she was going to do—nor would she delay a second. She was going to march right back to the school and demand to be allowed to see the Keller girls. She was not even going to wait for replies to the telegrams. She was going *now*. Annie Sullivan's fighting spirit had returned.

XXV. Preparation

Annie's determination carried her straight past the maid, who obviously had been given instructions to keep her out. "I'm going to Helen and Mildred even if Mr. Gilman himself is guarding their room!" She pushed the maid aside and marched up the stairs.

There was no one guarding the girls' room, and neither of them had gone to classes.

"I wouldn't leave Helen!" Mildred cried. "She didn't sleep all night and she hasn't eaten since you left. That old Mr. Gilman! He tried to get us to go to his house last night to stay, but Helen told him she wouldn't even go out of this room without you." Mildred was sobbing furiously, her anger, her fright, and her relief at seeing Annie all evident in this outburst. Helen was white and still. She just clung to Annie, and Annie could feel such tenseness in her every muscle that it frightened her.

"Helen, Helen darlin', it's going to be all right," she soothed. With an arm around either girl, she led them to the bed where the three sat huddled together as Annie told them about the telegrams. "I'm sure someone will come today," she ended.

Someone did. When early in the afternoon there was

an imperious knock at the door they clung together in fright.

"Shall I go?" Mildred asked.

Annie nodded. "If it's Mr. Gilman, though . . ." She got up and started after Mildred, with Helen still clinging to her arm. If it was Mr. Gilman he wasn't going to get even his foot inside that door! The strength of ten women surged up in her. She was ready to hurl herself against the door.

But it was not Mr. Gilman. It was Mr. Chamberlin.

At sight of him the strength drained out of Annie, and she began to tremble.

Perhaps he had talked to Kate Keller. Perhaps she actually did want Annie to leave Helen! Annie could not speak. Mildred had to do the talking for the three of them.

"Now, first, I want to know just what happened," said Mr. Chamberlin. Mildred poured out the story.

When she had finished, he said just two sentences. "You stay here. I'll talk to Gilman."

The sternness of his tone and the grimness of his face gave Annie courage again. "He's a very influential man," she told the girls. "He could ruin Mr. Gilman and his Cambridge School for Young Ladies if he was a mind to. Everybody reads his 'Listener' column."

It wasn't long until Mr. Chamberlin returned. He was alone.

"Annie, start packing your things—all of your things,"

he said. "I'm going to take you to the farm with me."

"*All* of us?" Annie asked.

"Certainly."

She did not ask what had transpired between him and Mr. Gilman. She simply started packing.

So it was at Red Farm that Mr. Hitz, sent immediately by Dr. Bell when he received Annie's telegram, found them that night—all three in a state of near collapse now that they were in the hands of friends and could relax. "We won't even talk about this till morning," Mr. Hitz said.

In the morning they learned that Mrs. Keller was on her way to them. After a night's sleep, and with this news to cheer them, they felt much less as if the good earth had slipped out from under their feet. Annie suggested a winter's walk in the woods. Mr. Hitz accompanied them, his long black cape flowing out behind him and his white beard whipped by the wind. The little Chamberlins ran ahead, gamboling in the new-fallen snow. Annie thought, "What a gay group we must look! Quite a contrast to the huddle of misery we three were when Mr. Chamberlin found us yesterday." The fright of the near-tragedy still constricted her own heart and an icy chill, which she knew was not caused by the wind, seemed to permeate her whole being. It was the result, she knew, of the words of Mrs. Keller's telegram to Mr. Gilman. Though she tried to disguise her feelings, she knew that she could not be relieved until she saw Kate Keller.

The days seemed to pass interminably for Annie.

When Mrs. Keller arrived she had already been to see Mr. Gilman. Annie knew the moment she stepped inside the Chamberlins' house that there was nothing to fear.

"Annie! Annie, my dear," Kate Keller said, taking Annie into her arms. "I didn't mean the telegram the way Mr. Gilman took it. Surely you know that."

"Yes," Annie murmured.

"I *was* giving him permission to make decisions, but I meant studies and amount of work, and even that was wrong of me. I thought he was a man and would have better judgment than I. But I never once thought of his sending you away. You must believe that."

They were both crying.

"It's all right now," Annie gulped.

"But what I made you go through! I'm so sorry, so ashamed of myself. The difficulty some of us with five senses and a certain intelligence have in communicating . . . Then when one thinks of what you've done with Helen, it . . . No one knows better than I that you are Helen's very life."

Annie remembered times when she hadn't gotten her exact meaning across—specifically, when she had insisted that Helen was her pupil and not a regular student at Perkins. She was aware, too, of the betwixt-and-between position of women and the resentment some men had if they did not have total control of a situation.

"Mr. Gilman didn't like me," Annie said. "This was

his golden opportunity to get rid of me. I know that."

Mrs. Keller sighed. Arm and arm she and Annie followed the others into the Chamberlins' pleasant big living room.

"He kept writing that Helen was a physical wreck, that she was on the verge of a nervous breakdown." Kate Keller stopped to peer critically at her daughter. "She certainly doesn't look wasted with illness to me."

"If she's more nervous than usual it's mostly his doing," Annie put in.

"He nearly gave all three of us nervous breakdowns," Mildred said grimly.

"I left no doubts in the gentleman's mind as to the future," Mrs. Keller assured them.

This was what Annie had been waiting most to hear.

"I said, 'I thank you kindly for what you did for Mildred, but I am withdrawing both girls from your school—officially—now. They will not return, ever.'"

The next question, of course, was what to do now.

"I suppose you still want to continue your preparation for college?" Mrs. Keller asked Helen. Annie found herself almost wishing Helen would say no, but she of course said "Yes," as Annie had known she would.

"Dr. Bell sent his suggestion that you complete the work with a private tutor rather than attempting another school," Mr. Hitz said.

Annie sighed with relief.

"Mr. Chamberlin and I want to extend our most

cordial invitation for Helen and Annie to stay with us as long as they wish," Mrs. Chamberlin said. "They both enjoy the farm, and we enjoy them. They need a little peace and quiet to recover from this horrible experience."

"That's very kind of you," Mrs. Keller said. Annie beamed her appreciation. There was no place she felt more accepted than in the home of the Chamberlins.

Mrs. Keller took Mildred back to Tuscumbia, and Annie began the rigorous task of finding a proper tutor for Helen. Mrs. Hutton sent word that the fund which had been set up for the education of Helen Keller was definitely for the support and maintenance of Annie Sullivan as well, that she had complete confidence in Annie's judgment, and that when Annie had secured a suitable tutor his fees would be paid.

It was not an easy task to find someone who could and would undertake the difficult job. At last, however, Annie found a man she thought would be satisfactory and who was willing to try. His name was Merton Keith, and he lived in Boston.

For the rest of that school year and through the following summer, Annie and Helen stayed on at Red Farm. Until June, Mr. Keith came out to them for Helen's lessons. Again Annie spelled every word into Helen's hand. At last, Mr. Keith began to get some understanding of mathematics through to Helen. "I'm glad it's beginning to mean something to *her*," Annie said. "I'm sure it never will to me."

Only because Helen had set her heart on going to college could Annie endure the exhausting, three-hour, tutoring sessions.

But the summer was sheer delight! King Philip's Pond was their perpetual playground. They swam; they picnicked; they boated.

"I wish this could go on forever," Annie thought.

The autumn came, however, as autumns do. With reluctance, Annie bade the Chamberlins goodbye and went to find living quarters for herself and Helen in Boston. When they were settled Mr. Keith took up the lessons again. And Annie took up the drudgery.

She never quite knew how she got through that year. It was the hardest one yet. Five days a week, via her own finger tips and Helen's palm, she transferred to Helen's brain the endless knowledge Mr. Keith felt she must have before the final entrance examinations, which she was going to take in June. English history, French, Latin, literature, more Greek, more mathematics—Annie felt like a sieve through which all this was being sifted. At times she had no idea what the substance of "this" was— words, figures; figures, words. So much had gone through the sieve that sometimes she felt sure its fine mesh would give away completely.

June, 1899, came, however, and the examinations and Helen's nineteenth birthday. Not for a moment had Annie Sullivan failed Helen Keller.

XXVI. Disappointment

June 29 and 30! June 29 and 30! It seemed to Annie that these dates were the points of a thousand tiny spears that were being hurled relentlessly and endlessly by a thousand little devils whose aim was true. They never missed. Over and over they pierced her temples until at times she thought she would go mad.

"If only I can get Helen through these examinations," she kept telling herself, "then I'll have another operation if they insist. I'll do anything to get rid of this pain. But, first, *I must get Helen through these examinations!*"

Little did she realize that she was not to be allowed to see her through them—that she was, in fact, not to be allowed to see her at all during the examinations.

Annie opened the letter from Radcliffe that contained the news: "It will be required that a complete stranger read the examinations to Miss Keller. Miss Sullivan is not to accompany her. This, we feel, would be giving Miss Keller an unfair advantage."

"We might have known that they'd have none of me," Annie sighed. "But who'd have thought they'd insist on a *stranger?* At least they let you have Mr. Gilman, someone who knew you, on the preliminaries."

"Well, I'm sure we don't want Mr. Gilman!" Helen replied indignantly.

Annie only paced the floor, her hands to her head.

The person who was finally found to do the job could not read the examinations to Helen, however, for he could not use the finger alphabet. Mr. Vining was a teacher at Perkins Institute, but one whom Annie and Helen had never met, so he fulfilled the requirement of "stranger." He could write Braille and would "transcribe" the questions. Helen would read them in Braille and write the answers on the typewriter. This "long way 'round" sounded to Annie like a distinct disadvantage to Helen, and she railed against circumstance. At last, however, she was forced to admit that if that was the way it had to be, that was the way it had to be.

When Helen left for Cambridge and her two-day ordeal, Annie sat down to wait it out. She found, however, that she could not sit still for more than a minute at a time. "I'll wear this carpet out," she thought. "Oh, I wish she'd never tried it! I wish she'd never gotten this college business into her head. If she does make it, dear Lord, give me strength to get through the next four years —or longer. It may take her more time to complete her college work than it takes others. Oh, my head! If I go completely blind again, I'll be after destroyin' meself. I swear I will. It won't be like the time by the river when Mr. Gilman had turned me out and I almost did it. The only good I am to anyone in the world is to Helen. If I found I could no longer be her eyes I'd not want to live."

Annie was sure the clock ticked more slowly those days than it had ever ticked before. The hands seemed to crawl like drugged ants, in a slow, slow circle.

When finally, on the second afternoon, the hour hand reached four, the closing hour for the examinations, Annie took herself in hand. "I've got to clean up and meet her with a smile," she said to herself. "I can't let her know what these two days have been like for me. After all, she's the one that's been taking the examinations, and surely I should exhibit confidence in her."

She found that she *must* do this, for it was a vague, despondent girl whom she met at the door a few hours later.

One look at her and Annie turned brisk again. "You did fine, of course!" she said. "Now tell me all about it. I can hardly wait."

"It was horrible," Helen answered dully.

"Oh, it couldn't have been that bad! I'll get you some hot tea. That will make you feel better." Annie patted the shoulder of the dejected girl who had slumped limply into a chair. Actually, she was alarmed. This wasn't like Helen at all.

"What happened?" she asked brightly when she returned. "Couldn't that Mr. Vining keep up with you?"

Helen shook her head. "It wasn't that. It was that American Braille of his. And in mathematics . . ." Her voice trailed off.

"It *was* bad for you that he didn't know the English Braille system, when you're so much more familiar with it," Annie said, thoughtfully. "But I'm just sure you did well, even with that handicap. You always do well, Helen."

"No, really, Teacher, the marks didn't even make sense to me in mathematics. You know how hard I'd worked to learn the American Braille signs, but I just couldn't remember them—in the algebra, I mean. I couldn't even understand the problems."

The waiting game the two played for the next few days was no fun for either of them. When the postman at last brought the stiff white envelope with the Radcliffe return, Annie thought, "Oh, it looks so formidable! I simply can't open it."

As usual, though Helen was at her side the minute the mail arrived, waiting eagerly for her to sort it.

"Did it come? Did it come?" Helen cried, excitedly.

Unsteadily, Annie answered, "Yes."

"Open it! Hurry!"

Annie's hands shook. She had trouble getting the enclosure out of the envelope, but the minute she saw it she realized why it had seemed so stiff and unyielding. It was a certificate of admission. Without stopping to spell a word to Helen she caught her in her arms, hugged her tight, and whirled her around the room in a wild highland fling.

Helen threw back her head and laughed aloud, dancing in gay abandon. She did not need a word. Teacher's actions spoke plainly enough.

At last Annie stopped, breathless. "It's a certificate of admission," she said. "Here. Feel it." It was in embossed letters, and Helen could feel the letters. "And at the bottom," Annie explained, "it says, 'Miss Keller passed with credit in Advanced Latin.' "

Helen "put on" a face. "You notice it wasn't mathematics," she said.

"That's all right. You passed in mathematics. You'd have had to, to be admitted. They certainly weren't granting you any special favors!"

Annie couldn't help feeling a little bitterness toward Radcliffe, for she felt the college authorities had made things unnecessarily difficult for Helen. But Helen had shown them! This was their day of triumph, Helen's and hers. It had been worth it after all.

Annie's small taste of bitterness was to become an entire mouthful when she accompanied Helen the following week on a call to the office of Miss Agnes Irwin, the Dean of Radcliffe. They went at Miss Irwin's request, Helen all eagerness to learn about her enrollment for the fall. Annie somewhat reluctantly now that the initial thrill of Helen's success with the examinations had worn off.

It was clear to Annie after five minutes in the presence of Dean Irwin that she had summoned Helen to dissuade her from entering the college.

"You have shown the world now that you can do it.

You passed the examinations," she said to Helen, through Annie. "Don't you think that is enough?"

Annie saw Helen pale and felt anger begin to rise in her own breast.

"But . . . But I took the examinations . . . I worked so hard—so hard so that I could go to college. That's the only reason I took them."

"It seems to me," said Dean Irwin, "since you have already made a start in a writing career, that you would rather put your time into writing than into struggling in the hopes of eventually obtaining a degree—hopes which might be vain, you know."

"They would not be 'vain hopes,'" Annie put in indignantly, even as she spelled Miss Irwin's words into Helen's hand. "Even with her handicaps, Helen can do any academic work that anyone else can do."

The interview was indeterminate, though Annie and Helen both left with a perfect understanding of the fact that Radcliffe did not want Helen Keller as a student.

Helen's lip was trembling as they left the Dean's office. Annie's arm went around her shoulder.

"What's the matter with Cornell or the University of Chicago?" Annie asked stanchly. "They both want you. We know that for they've both written asking you to consider them."

"But . . . But . . . It's Radcliffe I want. It's Radcliffe."

"So if it's Radcliffe you want, it's Radcliffe you're going to have," declared Annie with determination, forgetting for the moment her own dread of four more years of the grueling labor which Helen's attendance at any educational institution meant for Annie Sullivan.

XXVII. Summer's Respite

Annie did a great deal of thinking. She must talk to Dr. Bell and Mr. Hitz about this—and Mrs. Hutton. The money for Helen's education and for Helen's and Annie's support was coming entirely now from the fund Mrs. Hutton had set up.

Out of all her thinking, a plan for the summer began to take shape in Annie's mind. Certainly Helen needed a vacation. She herself must, without fail, give her eyes a rest if she expected them to see Helen through college, whatever and whenever it might be. Both of them loved Wrentham. Both of them loved the water. Why not rent a cottage at Wrentham for the summer, and simply relax and enjoy life for a change? With problems looming so large for the future, wouldn't it be wise to have a brief respite? The very thought of such a possibility seemed to release her from tension, to give her wings.

So the first question she asked Mrs. Hutton was not about college for Helen, but a cottage for the summer.

"Why, of course!" Mrs. Hutton said, with enthusiasm. "Annie, I want you to understand that the committee respects your judgment and fully expects that you shall make the decisions concerning the use of the funds made available. You have to live somewhere during the summer. Why shouldn't you live at Wrentham? I think it would do you both good."

Annie could hardly wait to tell Helen.

"How would you like to spend the summer at Wrentham?" she asked her, almost the minute she was inside the door.

Helen's face lighted up. "You mean at Red Farm?"

"I mean in a cottage of our own where we could do just as we pleased—have company. Perhaps your mother and Mildred and Phillips would come for a while."

"Oh, Teacher, that would be wonderful! And we could sail and swim to our hearts' content. *Could* we?"

"If I can find a cottage that we can rent reasonably we not only *can*, but we're going to."

Annie thought, as she looked at Helen's radiant face, what a very attractive young woman her pupil had become. And what of her teacher? Annie's thoughts went on—for one thing, she's not getting any younger, and for another, her eyes are getting no better. Oh, well! Give her a summer on the shore of one of Wrentham's lakes and she will not worry too much about such things. She's just going to enjoy herself!

She found a cottage on Lake Wollomonapoag which give her the delightfully warm feeling of coming home. She took it on the spot and wandered about inside, whistling. She stood in the middle of the living room, imagining how it would be on cool evenings with a fire in the fireplace and friends gathered in front of it, and good talk. She went out on the porch and stood looking over the lake, fringed with fragrant pines and dotted here and there with tiny green islands. She took a long, deep breath, drawing the fragrance into her lungs.

"I feel better already," she thought.

She took one more turn through the rooms, then went out, locked the door behind her, and dropped the key into her pocket. Eager as she was to get back and tell Helen of her find, she was reluctant to leave. "I haven't felt this way," she mused, "as if a place were really *mine* since Helen and I moved into the little vine-covered garden house after I first went to Tuscumbia." She laughed aloud, thinking what a turbulent "home" the cottage had been at first, but what a wonderful beginning it had represented—actually the beginning of life for Helen and, in a way, for her too. For what other life existed for Annie Sullivan save that which brought the world to Helen Keller? "Twelve years," she thought. "What a long time and what a short time! What joys and what sorrows!"

She sighed for she knew she must get busy on the Radcliffe problem. Ups and downs—they certainly constituted the story of her life. Little did others know of the turmoil within her, a storm which was never entirely stilled and which frequently erupted into violent blows of hurricane proportions!

Helen was at the door to meet her when she got back.

"Did you find one?" she demanded.

Annie did not answer. She put the key in Helen's hand.

"You did, and you love it!" Helen cried. "I can tell by the way you feel. And I'll love it, too. Oh, I can hardly wait! How soon can we move in?"

"As soon as we can get packed."

The key that Annie put into Helen's hand that day in early June proved to be the key to the happiest of summers.

Annie made frequent trips in to Boston for treatments on her eyes and began to know relief from the pain she had been fighting and from the fear which had been haunting her. This relief, plus the gaiety which Kate Keller and her two younger children brought to the cottage at Wrentham, set the stage for a perfect summer.

There was just one worry at the back of Annie's mind to mar the perfection, and she was sure that Helen thought about it too, though she said little. This, of course, was the problem of what to do about college.

Much of the time she succeeded in pushing this into a sufficiently remote corner of her mind so that she could forget it. Certainly the exhilarating swims, the tandem bicycle rides through the paths in the woods with Helen, the joyous picnics with the Kellers and the Chamberlins and other friends, the pleasant excursions by row boat and sailboat, and the quiet charm of canoeing left little time or place for worry.

One sunny afternoon, however, when Annie and the

Kellers were on their own private beach and the summer was getting on, Annie could no longer push her problem out of her mind. It kept nagging at her. "I have to do something," she thought. "Much as I'd like to go on this way forever, I'd be letting Helen down." Helen and Phillips and Mildred were in the water. Annie had been sitting on the warm sand with Mrs. Keller. She got up suddenly and plunged into the lake, starting immediately to swim out, away from the others. The merest suggestion of a plan had come to her, and she wanted to think about it.

She was a strong swimmer and often swam to the first little island. She headed in its direction, thinking, "I wonder if it would be possible to make some kind of arrangement with Radcliffe whereby Helen could study the same courses the freshmen would be studying in the college but not attend classes. Do it with a tutor. Perhaps we could even get the assignments from the professors." Looking up, she noticed that her island was not before her. There was considerable wind that day, and with her mind occupied, she had given no heed to the fact that it had altered her usual course. She was beginning to tire, and she was even farther from the island than she was from shore. She turned on her back and rested, still thinking about her plan. "I guess I'd better head back," she thought after a little. "That wind is really turning into quite a gale."

She soon realized that fighting her way back was not

going to be easy. She had swum out farther than she had realized, and now the wind had shifted slightly so that it was blowing straight from the shore and she must swim directly against the waves which it was hurling at her with increasing force. Still she was not afraid. In fact, there was something challenging and exhilarating about the struggle. She swam and rested, swam and rested.

As she watched the shore, however, she realized she was making little headway toward it. The moving, toy-sized figures seemed to grow no larger. "Well, Annie Sullivan," she said to herself, "you may well have yourself in a pretty pickle." But surely she was making some progress. There was nothing to do but keep trying.

She forced herself to rest between tries. She counted her strokes and tried to keep them even, with a steady pull.

It was becoming increasingly difficult to breathe. Her arms and legs ached. She caught herself gasping for breath, flailing her arms and legs.

Once she had thought of water and the death it held as friends; now she battled against them for life.

"This will never do!" she thought. "The next thing I know, I'll be going under."

Just then a big wave completely submerged her. When she came up her lungs seemed bursting with their need for air. For the first time she knew fear. Perhaps she *wasn't* going to make it! How stupid to get herself into this predicament! She tried to be calm, to tread water and keep her head above the waves until she could get enough air into her lungs to breathe normally. Then she tried again. Her strength was almost gone. So this was going to be the end of Annie Sullivan!

A little prayer took form in her mind and repeated itself over and over, "Take care of Helen. Please take care of Helen, God. Please."

Suddenly she thought she heard her name. "Annie!" Had she crossed into the other world? She blinked. No, there was the lake, the waves still coming at her with a vengeance. But something else was coming toward her. She took heart and tried the harder to keep her head above water. Surely she had seen a boat!

The next thing she knew strong arms were hoisting her over the side into a row boat and, before she lost consciousness she heard Phillips' voice, high with excitement. "Teacher, we couldn't see you! We thought you'd drowned!"

XXVIII. Radcliffe

The next day Annie was no worse for her experience, but she was sobered by it.

"Don't ever swim out that far again!" Helen ordered her sternly.

Seeing the concern in Helen's face, she said, "For your sake, I will never again take *any* such foolish risk. It was selfish and unthinking."

"Why, if Phillips hadn't missed you when he did—and Mother hadn't found those men right away to row the 'Naiad' to look for you, you—you wouldn't be here!" Helen started to cry.

"But they *did* rescue me and I *am* here, so let's dry those tears and forget it. Teacher was stupid. She won't be again; I promise you."

It would be a good time, she thought, to broach the subject she had been pondering when she got herself into yesterday's predicament. It would take Helen's mind off the harrowing experience.

As she launched into her proposed plan she watched Helen's face, and she knew at once that this was the right thing to do.

All of them hated to see summer end, the four Kellers

and Annie—Annie most of all. She had laid her plans as projected. She and Helen would go back to town for the winter. Helen would be tutored in the regular freshman subjects which she would take were she enrolled at Radcliffe. Annie had talked this over with Dean Irwin, and she had approved; she had even co-operated. "Anything, so long as they don't have to be bothered with Helen as a student!" Annie thought bitterly.

Yet Helen seemed pleased.

Annie thought she knew why; the reason was something that had been in the back of her own mind all along, but she had not mentioned it to Helen. Perhaps if Helen showed that she could do the work successfully this year, there would still be a chance of admission to Radcliffe later.

So Helen went back to studying and Annie went back to reading to her.

Before the winter was over Helen confessed what Annie had been sure she had in mind. "Teacher," she said one night, "do you think it would do any good for me to apply to Radcliffe again? Do you suppose they might take me *next* year?"

"It can do no harm to try," Annie said promptly. "Just don't get your hopes too high."

Annie had already talked to Dr. Bell and to Mrs. Hutton about this possibility, and they had both promised to do what they could.

At length she helped Helen compose the letter. They

would send it to the chairman of the academic board of Radcliffe:

Dear Sir:

As an aid to me in determining my plans for study the coming year, I apply to you for information as to the possibility of my taking the regular courses in Radcliffe College.

Since receiving my certificate of admission to Radcliffe last July, I have been studying with a private tutor. . . .

The conditions under which I work require the presence of Miss Sullivan, who has been my teacher and companion for thirteen years, as an interpreter of oral speech and as a reader of examination papers. In college she . . . would of necessity be with me in the lecture room and at recitations. I should do all of my written work on a typewriter. . . .

Is it possible for the College to accommodate itself to these unprecedented conditions, so as to enable me to pursue my subjects at Radcliffe?

The letter went off on May 5, and again Annie watched Helen suffer agonies in waiting—and suffered with her. A month went by and they heard nothing—two months. Annie wrote to Mr. Hitz, to Mrs. Hutton. At long last, though with little enthusiasm, Radcliffe agreed to let Helen, at the age of twenty, enroll with the Freshman Class in the fall of 1900.

"So at last we're here. At last you're a Radcliffe girl!" Annie announced, standing in the middle of the living room in the little house into which they had moved. "Now would you mind telling me, Miss Helen Keller, why it *had* to be Radcliffe?"

Helen giggled. "Because they didn't want me."

"That's what I thought," Annie said wryly.

She took up the old, grueling labor without complaint. Outwardly, she was gay. Helen had been elected vice-president of her class, and her classmates, as well as their old friends in Cambridge, came often to their little house for pleasant weekend evenings. Though Annie enjoyed this part of their life, she certainly did not enjoy the business at hand! Again she was haunted with the old fear that Helen couldn't really do this colossal task she had set for herself. More than anything in the world, she wanted her pupil to succeed, but the doubts in her mind would not be denied.

"I don't know what this Professor Copeland thinks he's trying to do," Annie complained to their friend Lenore Kinney one night, "unless it's to help some other people around here discourage Helen till she'll give up and quit."

"Why? What's Copey done now?" Lenore asked.

"Oh, he criticizes her composition unmercifully. That's the one field—that and her foreign languages—in which I've always felt she excelled. Now this 'Copey,' as you call him, is destroying all the confidence that I worked so hard to build up after 'The Frost King' fiasco."

"Well, maybe he has a reason," Lenore said.

Annie thought about that remark the next time one of Helen's compositions came back. She was reading into Helen's palm what "Copey" had written on her paper. Suddenly she paused.

"What is it?" Helen asked. "Isn't there more?"

"Yes," Annie said. "He says, 'Why don't you write about yourself, your own life and experiences, Miss Keller? I believe your writing would then be more sincere and less artificial.' You know, Helen, he may have a point there."

From then on Helen began getting better grades on her compositions, and Annie could see why. They did ring more true, now that she was writing about matters within her personal province.

One day when Annie and Helen were in Latin class there was a knock at the door. "Miss Sullivan, it is someone to see you and Miss Keller," the professor said.

Surprised and a little startled, Annie relayed the message to Helen, and they went out. "It's some man to see you on business," the girl who had come to get them reported. "He's in the next office. You can see him there."

A stranger arose as they entered, and Annie found herself instinctively preparing for battle. It seemed to her that so often these people who came to see Helen were there to exploit her in some way, wanting to use her name, wanting to interview her, wanting her to back some "good cause." And Helen, Annie felt, was far too gullible.

"Miss Sullivan?" the stranger said. "I'm William Alexander from *The Ladies' Home Journal*. And this is Miss Keller?"

"Yes," Annie said coolly. "Helen, this is Mr. Alexander from *The Ladies' Home Journal*," she spelled to Helen.

Helen smiled and put out her hand.

"It's an honor to meet you both," Mr. Alexander said, but Annie did not thaw. "Won't you sit down? I'm here to represent Mr. Bok, the editor of our magazine."

Annie's expression was cold. Another interview. She hated them.

"Yes, Mr. Alexander?" she said crisply.

"He would like to have Miss Keller write the story of her life to be run serially in *The Ladies' Home Journal*."

The coldness left Annie's eyes. She spelled the message into Helen's hand.

"The story of my life?" Helen asked, excitedly.

"Yes," said Mr. Alexander, pressing his advantage. "He authorized me to offer her $3,000 for it. Would you tell Miss Keller this, please?"

Annie's heart had begun to beat wildly. Three thousand dollars! It sounded like a fortune. But the work, the time . . .

"Oh, I—I don't know," she said to Mr. Alexander, as she spelled the message into Helen's hand. "She's very busy with her studies."

Helen did not hesitate, however. "Yes! Yes! Tell him

236

we'll do it. Tell him we'll try anyway. Oh, what a wonderful lot of money!"

"But, Helen."

"We can do it. I know we can, Teacher!"

"What did she say?" asked Mr. Alexander.

Annie sighed. "She said what she always says, 'We can do it!'"

"Good! Fine! I have the contract right here."

Now they were launched on two major projects—trying to keep up with the class assignments and writing a book —for a book, it soon became obvious, was what was expected of them.

"I can use my themes I've done for Professor Copeland," Helen had said lightly. It was plain to Annie, however, that these would constitute only a very small part of a complete autobiography.

"You'll have to begin at the beginning," she said.

Very soon they learned that magazines have deadlines that must be met. For the first installment Mr. Bok wanted five thousand words, and he must have them by a certain date. That certain date loomed very large to Annie. They did not dare neglect the studies or Helen would fall behind in her classes, and that would never do. "It would be just the excuse they're waiting for to get rid of her," Annie said desperately to Lenore Kinney.

They worked night and day, and they made the deadline for the first installment.

"This is only the beginning!" Annie wailed. "For the

life of me I just don't see how we can go on with it!"

"But we signed a contract," Helen reminded her.

"So we did," Annie sighed, not admitting how badly her eyes were hurting.

Lenore Kinney saw how impossible the situation was. One evening when she came in Annie saw at once that she had something she was bursting to tell them. "Do you girls think you could use some competent help?" she asked almost immediately.

"You aren't about to offer your services, are you?" Annie chided her.

"Well, hardly; but I am about to offer you somebody else's—and that somebody has had experience as an editor."

"What?" Annie cried, almost afraid to believe.

"In fact, he's doing editorial work for *The Youth's Companion* right now, and doing some teaching at Harvard, and he writes, and. . . ."

"Wait a minute," Annie interrupted. "He sounds as busy as we are. What makes you think he'd help us?"

"Because I've already talked to him, and he said he'd come over and talk to you tomorrow. His name's John Macy."

XXIX. John Macy

John Macy came the following Sunday afternoon. He was a quiet, nice-looking, intelligent young man, and he knew his business. He found Annie and Helen in a scramble of papers, Annie looking distraught and frustrated, Helen pecking doggedly away at the typewriter.

"Look!" Annie fairly shouted at him. "Notes in Braille. Themes in typescript. And besides what's here, ideas in her head. We've no organization, no pattern. We don't know where we're going. And the magazine is screaming for copy for the next installment. They have to have it before they can go to press!"

John Macy smiled. "Now if you will just show me where the first installment left off, and what you have done beyond that . . ."

He stayed all afternoon and evening. Before he left Annie could see the pattern of the second installment, and she felt a relief comparable only to that she had known when Helen had passed her entrance examinations.

At the door, John took Annie's hand. "It will come out all right," he said. "And, Anne, I think it would be well if you would teach me the manual alphabet. Then

I can remove from your shoulders some of the load of spelling the manuscript back to Helen."

Annie looked at him gratefully, but her usually glib tongue found no words to express her gratitude. No one had ever called her "Anne" before.

After John Macy came into their lives things were different in the little house. Though work still filled the days and the weeks to brimming, it seemed less burdensome to both Annie and Helen. The order that he established from the chaos of the writing project, in itself, gave Annie a peace of mind that helped tremendously. But there was something else. There was the pleasure of John's visits to look forward to when the days grew long and tedious with study, with the constant spelling, spelling, spelling which Annie did day after day after day. For Annie liked John Macy, and John liked Anne.

The fact that he called her "Anne," alone, did something for her. The feeling it gave her was akin to that which Dr. Bell had always evoked, a feeling that she was a person in her own right, a person worthy of respect.

One night when they had finished with work and were roasting chestnuts in the fireplace, John said, "Anne, you're the most amazing person! Here you sit, day after day, performing the feat of this age—literally spelling a blind-deaf girl through college—after bringing her out of an absolute prison of noncommunication—and yet you seem to want no credit or acclaim."

Instead of answering him, she asked a question. "Why

do you call me 'Anne'? Everyone else calls me 'Annie.'"

John threw back his head and laughed uproariously. "If that isn't typical!"

"But you didn't answer me."

John's eyes grew soft. "Because it fits you."

They got the second installment of Helen's *Story of My Life* off to the publisher—and the third, and fourth. Helen's first year at Radcliffe was drawing to a close.

"Is it as much fun as you thought it would be?" Annie asked her one night.

"It isn't fun at all," Helen admitted. "We don't have time for anything but work."

"The summer is coming," Annie said, cheerfully, "and we'll be back at Wrentham." She didn't ask if Helen wanted to come back to Radcliffe another year. She knew what the answer would be. Helen might not be having fun, but she had started something that she intended to finish—no matter what. And despite the drudgery of Annie's life as she helped her toward the goal, she would not have had her give it up. Annie Sullivan had a strength of will to match Helen's. This was one reason they had gotten on so well together for fourteen years.

So they came back, and John Macy helped them to complete the magazine material for which they had contracted. He even helped Annie read Helen's lessons to her whenever he could spare the time. "You're reading yourself blind," he scolded one night when he found Annie ill with one of her bad headaches.

"Well, it wouldn't be the first time," Annie managed to quip.

"You're incorrigible, Anne Sullivan, simply incorrigible!" John said, squeezing her hand.

Shortly after the magazine contract had been met another editor appeared. A man from a book-publishing firm called on Annie and Helen at their home.

"The Century Company would like to have Miss Keller expand her autobiography," he explained to Annie. "We would also like to have material on you and your part in this miraculous story. These two we would combine and publish in book form."

Annie answered a flat "No" to the second part of his request. "But I'll ask Miss Keller about the other," she told him.

Knowing now the work that went into writing, Helen was not as eager as she had been with *The Ladies' Home Journal* representative.

"Perhaps, during summer vacation . . ." she said, hesitantly. "What do you think, Teacher?"

"I think we'd better take a little time to think it over and let them know later."

Helen nodded vigorous approval.

After their caller had left Annie said, "What I really wanted was time to talk it over with John."

"Yes, he'll know the right thing for us to do," Helen agreed.

Annie told him the whole story, including what had

been asked of her personally. "The last we won't even consider," she ended, "but we would like your judgment on whether we should undertake to do Helen's *Life* over for them."

"If you will include me in your plans," he said, "I think we could do it very nicely during summer vacation, but I have a proviso."

"A proviso?" Annie looked at him in some surprise.

"Yes. That you let me edit your letters and the early accounts of teaching Helen which you wrote for the Perkins' Institute reports and, in this way, make up a section of the book to satisfy the publisher's request for material about you."

"I'll do no such thing!" Annie flared.

John only smiled. "I like you when you're angry," he said. "In fact, I like you any time. I love you, Anne. Will you marry me?"

XXX. *Reward*

Annie had trouble in believing that she had heard correctly. She had grown so accustomed to thinking of herself as only an adjunct to Helen Keller that she had ceased to consider a life of her own.

"I—I—why I *couldn't*. John, what are you saying?" she had stammered.

"I am saying that I love you and that I want to marry you."

For a quiet moment John Macy looked deep into the eyes of Annie Sullivan. His smile embraced her. Then he went away.

"What is it, Teacher?" Helen asked, sensing her agitation at once.

"John—John asked me to marry him. But he *couldn't* mean it!"

"Oh, Teacher, how wonderful! Of course he meant it!"

"But how *could* I? I couldn't leave you."

"I'm sure John didn't mean you should leave me."

Helen was right. As John discussed his plans with Annie he made this very clear.

"Of course I understand your feeling of responsibility to Helen. You are her very life. Separating you from her never entered my mind. She would be with us always."

"But would it be fair to you? You know all my time has been devoted to her."

"I know. I still want to marry you, Anne Sullivan."

He took her chin in his hand, tilted her head back, and kissed her.

Annie found John's arguments persuasive—both for putting her in the book and for marrying her. In his quiet way, he was masterful, and she found this very pleasant for a change. There was a restfulness about John, too, that affected Annie as did the soft wind sighing through the pines at Wrentham. He was good for her turbulent spirit. There were even times when she felt she was at peace. Then again there were times when she knew that she was not. Who was she to marry John Macy?

The book progressed steadily under John's sure guidance and with his excellent editing. He was working on Annie's letters now.

"How you stand out in these letters to Mrs. Hopkins!" he exclaimed one day. "Even if I'd never met you I would know you from these letters."

"And what would ye be knowin'?" Annie asked, her eyes sparking mischief.

He reached for her hand and pulled her to him. After a bit he said, "You're witty, Darling, clever, original, brilliant—but most of all, wise. I love you for all these things; I love you in all ways."

"Thank you, me Darlin'," she said humbly, "but ye

know I'm no such person at all. Sure an' ye know it. And if *ye* don't, *I* do."

She had asked. She had her answer. But she would not accept it.

"Do you want to know what I really am?" Annie asked, and without waiting for him to reply went on, "I'll tell you."

She started to pace the floor, her hands clasped behind her. She told him about her life as she first remembered it at Feeding Hills, her mother's dying, her father's coming home drunk night after night. She told him about Jimmie and Tewksbury and what Jimmie's death had done to her. She told him about her blindness and the terrible desire within her to go to school. Then about Perkins and how miserable a misfit she had been until Mrs. Hopkins came.

John didn't stop her. She stopped herself at last.

"Now ye know. Ye know what I *really* am."

She sank down on the settee in exhaustion. She was afraid to look at him until she heard his voice, tender yet firm. "I love you, Anne, more than ever."

The summer ended, and they somehow got through another school year. Now the book was behind them, but there still remained the long, hard pull of Helen's senior and most difficult year. Even with John's love to sustain her, Annie dreaded this with all her heart. She thought Helen approached it with somewhat the same feeling.

Yet, if she could make it, what a wonderful triumph it would be for both of them!

No matter how long the hours they spent, they seemed never to be able to finish the reading assignments. The thought of Helen's having to retain all the information that was being poured into her mind through the obtainable Braille books and through Annie's finger tips appalled Annie.

Relentlessly, June came on. Relentlessly, Annie's fingers talked—endlessly—endlessly—into Helen's palm. Relentlessly, the fear grew in Annie.

Then examination week was upon them, and Annie found herself in the same frantic state she had been in when Helen took her entrance examinations. Only this time the tension was even greater, for they were in the end zone, going for the goal. To Annie it seemed that this goal, win or lose, was the ultimate. Helen's failure or success in obtaining her degree would give Annie the answer to the two questions which had been with her day and night for seventeen years: was Helen Keller, with her handicaps of deafness and blindness, capable of being educated to the degree that a normal adult could be educated? Had Annie Sullivan, with her handicaps of birth and background, been capable of molding the mind of another human being to this extent? Annie had never been sure, and it seemed to her that in the resolution to these two questions lay the answer to the quest of her life. If Helen failed she had failed.

If Helen succeeded she had succeeded.
Helen succeeded.

The palms of Annie's hands were wet as she helped Helen dress for commencement. Helen could have been no more nervous than she.

"I remember my graduation from Perkins," she told Helen, "my *only* graduation." She remembered the scene in Tremont Temple in Boston nearly twenty years before. The pageant passed before her eyes—the "exercises" by the younger students, the military drills, the demonstrations, the well-rehearsed "special numbers." She remembered that they had been called "charming and quaint" by those who had come to stare. She remembered that aging Laura Bridgman had sat behind her on the platform and the attention of the audience had been distracted from the odd program to the even more curious finger conversation between Miss Bridgman and a friend. Even the governor had referred to the Perkins' commencement exercises as "entertainment," she thought wryly.

All this flashed through her mind, but she said only, "I had a white dress and a pink sash."

"I know you were beautiful, Teacher."

"They said I looked like Mrs. Cleveland."

"President Cleveland's wife?"

"Yes. But why did I bring that up? This is *your* day."

"*Our* day, dear Teacher."

Annie smiled, not only because of Helen's comment, but also because things were so different from that other day long ago.

Annie did not wear white today. She wore a plain black dress. She was to sit on the platform with Helen, and she wished to be as inconspicuous as possible among the ninety-six capped-and-gowned girls who made up the Radcliffe graduating class that June day in 1904.

As the graduation exercises proceeded Annie realized that her nervousness had left her. She was very glad that no special fuss was being made over Helen's graduation. She liked it this way. The name of Helen Adams Keller was listed on the fourth page of the Radcliffe commencement program, alphabetized with the other "cum laudes." The very normalcy of all this made it even more clear that Helen Keller and Annie Sullivan had reached their goal.

Helen held her sheepskin in one hand.

Taking her other hand in hers, Annie said, "Come. John is waiting for us."

The silent storm within her at last was stilled.